FROM CHAINS TO WINGS

A Poetry Revolution for Healing

• • •

THE WORKBOOK

*A companion to the book From Chains to Wings —
your personalized practice companion for recognizing patterns,
building awareness, and discovering choices*

• • •

Joy Stephenson-Laws, JD, Certified Holistic Health Coach

FROM CHAINS TO WINGS: THE WORKBOOK
A Poetry Revolution for Healing

Copyright © 2025 by Joy Stephenson-Laws

Workbook ISBN: 979-8-9939740-4-0
Main Book ISBN:979-8-9939740-1-9 (Paperback)
Main Book ISBN:979-8-9939740-0-2 (Hardcover)

First Edition: 2025
Printed in the United States of America

For permissions and information:
phlabs.org

IF YOU ARE IN CRISIS

If you are experiencing thoughts of self-harm or suicide, please reach out for help immediately:

National Suicide & Crisis Lifeline: Call or text **988**
Crisis Text Line: Text **HOME** to **741741**
Emergency Services: Call **911**

This workbook should not be used as crisis intervention. If you are in crisis, please seek immediate professional support.

WORKBOOK USE AGREEMENT

By using this workbook, you acknowledge and agree that:

- You are using these exercises at your own risk

- You will skip any exercise that increases your distress

- You will seek professional help if symptoms worsen

- You understand this is not therapy or medical treatment

- You will not hold the author or publisher liable for any outcomes

PRIVACY AND PERSONAL USE

This workbook is for your personal use only. Your written responses and reflections are private. You are never obligated to share your workbook content with anyone.

The workbook may not be reproduced or shared digitally without written permission from the publisher. Single photocopies of individual pages may be made for personal use only.

Note on Research References: While this workbook references various studies and therapeutic approaches, it represents the author's interpretation and practical application of these concepts. Scientific understanding of trauma and nervous system regulation continues to evolve. For the most current research and clinical applications, please consult recent peer-reviewed publications and qualified professionals.

Note on Examples: Names and identifying details in examples have been changed to protect privacy. Some examples are composites drawn from multiple experiences. Any resemblance to specific individuals is coincidental.

TABLE OF CONTENTS

PART THREE: RELATIONSHIPS AS PRACTICE

From inner awareness to outer relationships

Note: *This workbook is designed to be used alongside the main book "From Chains to Wings." Work at your own pace. Skip what doesn't resonate. Return to exercises as needed.*

FROM CHAINS TO WINGS
THE WORKBOOK

A Companion Guide for Your Practice

Joy Stephenson-Laws, JD

> *"You can read about swimming all you want, but at some point, you need to get in the water. This workbook is your practice pool—a safe place to experiment with awareness, notice your patterns, and track what you discover about your nervous system."*

What This Workbook Is

This workbook is your personal companion to *From Chains to Wings*. While the main book explains concepts and shares stories, this workbook gives you space to:

- **Practice** the exercises from each chapter

- **Track** your patterns as you notice them

- **Record** what works (and what doesn't) for your unique nervous system

- **Return** to exercises when patterns resurface

- **Document** your progress over time

Think of it as your lab notebook—a place to experiment, observe, and learn what's true for you.

How to Use This Workbook

The Basic Approach

1. **Read the main book chapter first** to understand the concepts

2. **Then turn to the corresponding workbook section** for practice

3. **Work at your own pace**—some exercises take minutes, others weeks

4. **Skip what doesn't resonate**—not every exercise fits every person

5. **Return as needed**—patterns cycle back, and that's normal

Important to Remember

- **You cannot fail these exercises**

- **Writing single words or fragments is perfectly fine**

- **Leaving sections blank is okay**

- **Your answers will change over time—that's progress**

- **Skip anything that increases distress**

- **This is YOUR record of YOUR patterns**

The Structure

This workbook follows the same three-part journey as the main book:

Part One: Recognizing Your Patterns (Chapters 1-4)

Building awareness of what your nervous system does

- Chapter 1: Noticing patterns without drowning
- Chapter 2: Understanding protection disguised as sabotage
- Chapter 3: Reading your body's signals
- Chapter 4: Finding one safe place when everything feels activated

In Part One, you're just observing. No pressure to change anything.

Part Two: Learning to Move (Chapters 5-8)

Working with what you notice

- Chapter 5: Recognizing capacity changes
- Chapter 6: Understanding when anxiety makes sense
- Chapter 7: Working with your night guard
- Chapter 8: Matching movement to your nervous system state

Now you'll add gentle experiments using the three-step pattern: Notice → Validate → Adjust

Part Three: Relationships as Practice (Chapters 9-13)

Awareness with others present

- Chapter 9: Recognizing boundary patterns
- Chapter 10: Understanding emotional syncing
- Chapter 11: Reading intensity as information
- Chapter 12: Identifying inherited patterns
- Chapter 13: Living with awareness without drowning in it

The advanced practice—maintaining awareness when other nervous systems are involved.

How to Approach Each Exercise

Each workbook chapter includes:

- **"Speaking It True" sections** - Simple truth statements about that chapter's pattern

- **Recognition exercises** - Helping you identify your specific patterns

- **Practice experiments** - Small things to try (not requirements)

- **Tracking spaces** - Places to note what you observe

- **Key takeaways** - The essential point to remember

A Note About "Success"

Success with this workbook looks like:

- Noticing one pattern you didn't see before

- Having three seconds of awareness during a triggered moment

- Recognizing a pattern AFTER it runs (still counts!)

- Being 1% kinder to yourself about your patterns

- Remembering you have choices, even if you can't use them yet

Success does NOT require: eliminating patterns, constant awareness, perfect boundaries, or feeling "healed."

Before You Begin

What You'll Need

- The main book *From Chains to Wings*

- This workbook

- A pen (pencil if you prefer to erase—but consider keeping your first answers visible)

- 5-10 minutes per exercise (though you can take longer)

- Permission to go slowly

- Compassion for yourself when patterns run anyway

When to Seek Additional Support

This workbook is not therapy or medical treatment. Please work with qualified professionals if you're experiencing:

- Severe anxiety or depression

- Trauma responses that feel overwhelming

- Thoughts of self-harm

- Symptoms that interfere with daily functioning

- Any medical or mental health crisis

Crisis Resources:
National Suicide & Crisis Lifeline: 988 | Crisis Text Line: Text HOME to 741741

Your Journey Starts Here

You're about to begin mapping your own nervous system—its patterns, protections, and possibilities. Some days you'll have profound insights. Other days you'll forget everything you've learned. Both are part of the process.

This workbook will be here whenever you need it. You can start and stop, skip sections, return to exercises months later. There's no perfect way to use it except the way that serves you.

Remember the Foundation

Notice first.
Validate second.
Only then try to adjust.

Your body needs acknowledgment before it will consider change.
Sometimes the acknowledgment alone is all you need.

• • •

You're not broken.
Your patterns make sense.
Awareness creates choice.
Even tiny amounts of awareness count.
Progress isn't linear.
You already have everything you need.

Let's begin.

• • •

Turn to Part One to start building awareness of your patterns.

PART ONE

Recognizing Your Patterns

Building awareness of what your nervous system does

My patterns aren't problems to fix.
They're protective strategies that once helped.

In Part One, I'm just noticing.
What patterns do I have?
When do they show up?
What might they be protecting?

That observation—that tiny space of awareness—
changes everything.

Not because it stops the patterns,
but because it reminds me:
I am more than my protective strategies.

What You'll Discover in Part One

You're either lost in a pattern or aware of it happening. There's no in-between.

When you're lost in checking locks, you ARE the checking. When anxiety floods, you ARE the anxiety. No separation exists between you and the experience.

But sometimes—mid-check, mid-panic—you catch yourself: *"I'm doing that thing again."*

That catch changes everything.

Not because the pattern stops. It doesn't. You still check the lock. The anxiety still floods. But now 10% of you observes while 90% experiences. That 10% is where choice lives.

• • •

Your Journey Through Part One

Chapter 1: You're Not Broken

Learn to distinguish having anxiety from being consumed by it. The difference between "I am anxious" and "I notice anxiety" creates space for choice.

Practice focus: Developing your observer capacity

Chapter 2: Your Inner Protector

Recognize when pulling back from good things might be wisdom, not self sabotage. Sometimes your body knows what your mind doesn't.

Practice focus: Noticing protective hesitation

Chapter 3: When Your Body Speaks

Notice where tension lives—jaw, shoulders, stomach. Physical symptoms often connect to emotional patterns, though the connections vary by person.

Practice focus: Body awareness and symptom tracking

Chapter 4: Finding One Safe Place

When everything feels activated, locate one neutral spot—an earlobe, a knee. This becomes your anchor.

Practice focus: Finding neutral zones when overwhelmed

• • •

How to Work with Part One Exercises

Remember these principles as you practice:

- **Just notice** – Don't try to change patterns yet

- **No judgment** – Patterns developed for good reasons

- **Start small** – Even 3 seconds of awareness counts

- **Expect forgetting** – You'll lose awareness often (normal!)

- **Notice after** – Catching patterns afterward still counts

- **Be patient** – Awareness builds slowly over time

Important: Part One asks you to notice, not fix. You'll want strategies immediately. Part Two provides them. But you can't change what you can't see clearly.

This frustrates some people. "I know my patterns," they say. But knowing about patterns and catching them mid-action are different skills. One is thinking. The other is recognizing yourself in real time.

• • •

Before You Begin the Exercises

Try this right now: Notice whether you're absorbed in reading or aware that you're reading. Can you do both? That split attention—reading while knowing you're reading—that's your observer developing.

If you could do it even for a moment, you're ready for Part One.

If you couldn't, that's okay too. The exercises will help you develop this capacity.

What "Success" Looks Like in Part One:

- *Noticing you checked the locks (even after the fifth check)*
- *Recognizing your shoulders are at your ears (even if you can't lower them)*
- *Catching yourself saying yes (even after the word is out)*
- *Finding one boring spot in your body that feels okay*
- *Having 3 seconds of "oh, I'm doing that pattern"*

That's it. That's enough. That's everything.

A Note on Resistance

You might feel resistance to "just noticing." Your mind might say:

- "This won't help anything"
- "I need to DO something about these patterns"
- "Awareness alone won't fix me"
- "I already know what my patterns are"

This resistance is normal. It's actually another pattern to notice: *"Oh, there's my impatience with just observing."*

Trust that awareness itself is powerful. Research shows that metacognitive awareness—simply noticing your thoughts and patterns—accounts for significant therapeutic change regardless of what techniques you use.

• • •

> ***Awareness comes first.***
> ***Understanding follows.***
> ***Change (if needed) comes later.***
>
> *For now, just notice.*

Turn the page to begin Chapter 1:
You're Not Broken Your journey into awareness starts with learning the difference between having patterns and being consumed by them.

CHAPTER 1 WORKBOOK

You're Not Broken: Finding Your Watcher

SPEAKING IT TRUE

When anxiety shows up (again):

Your mind says: *"I should be over this by now"*

Your body says: *"Danger! Check everything!"*

The truth: *"My body learned this long ago. It's still protecting me."*

Welcome to Your Chapter

If you keep thinking "Why am I still like this?" or "I should be past this by now" — you're exactly where you need to be.

Here's what we're going to do:

☐ Learn to watch your anxiety without fighting it

☐ Stop beating yourself up about having patterns

☐ Practice noticing (that's all — just noticing)

Time needed: 15 minutes to read, then quick practices through your day

Quick Check-In

Right now, notice your body. Where is it tight?

- ☐ Shoulders
- ☐ Jaw
- ☐ Chest
- ☐ Stomach
- ☐ Neck
- ☐ All over
- ☐ Can't tell

That tightness? It's just information. You don't need to fix it.

The Main Idea

Your anxiety isn't because you're weak. Your body learned to stay on guard to keep you safe. Maybe when you were young, things were:

- Unpredictable
- Scary sometimes
- Hard to understand

So your body learned: **"Always be ready. Always check. Never fully relax."**

Now it still does this, even when you're safe. Like a smoke alarm that screams at burnt toast.

The Timeline Truth

Fill in your story:

How long have you had anxiety? _____ years

How many times have you thought "I should be over this"?

☐ Every day

☐ All the time

☐ Right now

Here's the truth: There's no deadline for feeling better.

If your body protected you this way for 10 years, why would it stop in 10 days? Or even 10 months?

Your Daily Practice: Finding Your Watcher

The most important thing you'll learn: **The part of you that notices "I'm anxious" isn't anxious.**

Try This Now (30 seconds):

1. Notice that you're reading this page
2. Notice any feelings you have about it
3. Notice WHO is doing the noticing

That noticing part? That's your "watcher." It's calm. It just observes.

This Week's Simple Practice

Day 1-2: Just Notice One Thing

Pick ONE thing you do when anxious:

- ☐ Check locks multiple times
- ☐ Look for exits in rooms
- ☐ Check your phone constantly
- ☐ Tense your shoulders
- ☐ Other: _____

When you catch yourself doing it, just say inside: "Oh, there's my pattern."

Don't try to stop. Just notice.

Day 3-4: Notice the "Should" Voice

Count how many times you think "I should be over this":

Day	Morning	Afternoon	Evening
Day 3			
Day 4			

Day 5-6: Practice New Words

Instead of saying: "I'm anxious"

Try saying: "I'm having some anxiety" or "Anxiety is visiting"

Instead of: "I'm broken"

Try: "I have patterns that once kept me safe"

This isn't positive thinking. It's just more accurate.

Day 7: Look Back (Without Judging)

This week I noticed my pattern about _____ times.

The "should be over it" thought showed up _____ times.

One thing I learned:

Common "Should" Thoughts

Check any you've had:

- [ ] "Other people don't still have this problem"

- [ ] "I've tried everything, so why..."

- [ ] "It's been years since [bad thing], I should be fine"

- [ ] "Adults don't have these issues"

- [ ] "I'm being dramatic"

- [ ] "I'm weak"

- [ ] "I'm going backwards"

> **Every single person with anxiety has thought these things. You're not alone. You're not behind. There's no schedule.**

Your Permission Note

I give myself permission to:

- Still have this pattern

- Not be "over it" yet

- Take as long as I need

- Have good days and bad days

- Just notice instead of fix

- Be exactly where I am

Signed: _____

Date: _____

SPEAKING IT TRUE - End of Week

What actually happened:

My mind said: *"You should be better by now"*

My patterns: *Kept happening*

My watcher: *Started to notice both*

The truth: *Noticing is the whole practice*

Remember This Week

- Your patterns kept you safe once
- There's no timeline for healing
- The "watcher" part of you is always calm
- Noticing is enough — don't try to fix
- You're not broken or behind
- "Should" is just shame talking

Crisis Help

If things feel too big to handle alone:

- Call 988 (crisis line)
- Text HOME to 741741
- Talk to someone you trust

Next: Chapter 2 - Why You Pull Back from Good Things

(Only move on after practicing this chapter for at least 7 days)

CHAPTER 2 WORKBOOK

Your Inner Protector: Why You Wreck Good Things

SPEAKING IT TRUE - Good Things Feel Dangerous

When something good is about to happen:

Your mouth says: "This is great!"

Your body says: "RUN! GET OUT! DANGER!"

Your protector says: "We need to wreck this before it wrecks us"

The truth: "Good things turned bad before. My body remembers."

Welcome to Chapter 2

Have you ever:

☐ Gotten a great opportunity and immediately wanted to run?

☐ Had something good happen and thought "this won't last"?

☐ Pushed away someone who was kind to you?

☐ Ruined something right before it got really good?

If you checked any box, you have an inner protector. It's not trying to hurt you — it's trying to save you.

Quick Story

Joy gets offered a promotion at work. Here's what happens:

> **Boss:** "We want you to lead the team."
>
> **Joy's mouth:** "Thank you so much!"
>
> **Joy's body:** [Stomach drops, chest tightens]
>
> **Joy's thoughts later:** "I should turn it down. I'll fail. They'll see I'm not good enough."
>
> **Joy, two days later:** Calls in sick. Starts messing up on purpose.

Joy isn't sabotaging herself. Her protector is trying to save her from something.

Understanding Your Protector

Your inner protector learned that good things can be dangerous because:

- ☐ Success meant more pressure when you were young
- ☐ Being noticed meant being criticized
- ☐ Good times always ended badly
- ☐ Love came with conditions
- ☐ Standing out meant being a target
- ☐ Happiness meant something bad would follow

Your protector remembers all of this, even if you don't.

This Week's Practice: Meeting Your Protector

Day 1-2: Notice the Pull-Back

Watch for times you pull back from good things:

Good Thing That Happened	My First Thought/Feeling
Someone complimented me	
Got invited somewhere	
Something went well	
Someone was nice to me	

Just notice. Don't judge. Your protector has reasons.

Day 3-4: Track Your Protector's Moves

How does your protector try to "save" you?

- [ ] Makes you want to quit before you start
- [ ] Tells you "this won't last"
- [ ] Points out everything wrong
- [ ] Makes you feel sick or tired
- [ ] Reminds you of past failures
- [ ] Says "you don't deserve this"
- [ ] Creates problems out of nowhere

SPEAKING IT TRUE - Your Protection Pattern

Fill in what happens to you:

When [good thing] happens: _____

My mouth says: _____

My body feels: _____

My protector whispers: _____

What it's protecting me from: _____

Day 5-6: Talk to Your Protector

Have a conversation (yes, really):

> **You:** "Hey protector, I notice you showed up when [good thing] happened."
>
> **You:** "What are you worried will happen?"
>
> *Listen. The answer might surprise you.*
>
> **You:** "Thank you for trying to protect me from that."
>
> **You:** "That happened when I was _____ years old."
>
> **You:** "I'm _____ years old now. Some things are different."

Your protector might not believe you yet. That's okay. Keep talking.

Common Protector Fears

My protector is afraid that if good things happen:

- [ ] People will expect too much
- [ ] I'll be disappointed when it ends
- [ ] Others will be jealous or angry
- [ ] I'll be seen (and judged)
- [ ] I'll find out I'm not good enough
- [ ] I'll lose control
- [ ] Something bad will balance it out

These fears made sense once. Something taught your protector these lessons.

The Age Check

Think about your biggest protector fear. Now ask:

How old do I feel when this fear shows up? _____ years old

What was happening in my life at that age?

Your protector might be protecting the younger you, not current you.

Day 7: Working WITH Your Protector

Instead of fighting your protector, try this:

When protector shows up:

1. Notice it: "Oh, my protector is here"

2. Thank it: "Thanks for trying to keep me safe"

3. Check in: "Is this current danger or old danger?"

4. Reassure it: "I'm grown now. I can handle this differently"

5. Go slow: "We can take one tiny step and see what happens"

This week, I noticed my protector showed up _____ times.

It was trying to protect me from:

One thing I want to tell my protector:

SPEAKING IT TRUE - End of Week

What you learned:

Good things feel: *"Dangerous to my protector"*

My protector remembers: *"When good turned bad"*

My current truth: *"Some good things might actually be safe now"*

My practice: *"Thank my protector, then check if danger is real"*

Working With (Not Against) Your Protector

Remember:

- Your protector saved you once (maybe many times)
- It doesn't know time has passed
- Fighting it makes it stronger
- It needs updating, not defeating
- Small steps help it trust

This Week's Experiments

Choose ONE to try:

☐ Accept one small compliment without deflecting

☐ Let one good thing happen without predicting doom

☐ Stay present for one nice moment

☐ Tell someone one thing you're proud of

☐ Say yes to something small that feels good

If your protector freaks out, just notice. Say "I see you're worried. We're okay."

Common Protector Patterns

Which do you do?

The Pattern	This Is Me
Ghost people when they get too close	☐
Quit right before succeeding	☐
Get "sick" before big opportunities	☐
Pick fights when things are going well	☐
Mess up on purpose	☐
Push away compliments	☐
Never celebrate wins	☐

These aren't character flaws. They're protection strategies.

Your Permission Note

I give my protector permission to:

• Keep protecting me

• Be suspicious of good things

• Take time to trust

• Warn me about dangers (real or remembered)

• Learn slowly that some things are safe now

I give myself permission to:

• Take tiny steps toward good things

• Thank my protector without obeying it

• Check if danger is current or old

Signed: _____

Remember This Week

- Self-sabotage is really self-protection
- Your protector has good reasons (even if they're old reasons)
- Fighting your protector makes it fight harder
- Thanking it calms it down
- Small steps help build trust
- You're not broken for protecting yourself
- Good things can be safe (sometimes)

Crisis Help

If your protector is keeping you from everything good:

- Call 988 (crisis line)
- Text HOME to 741741
- Talk to a counselor who understands trauma
- Remember: Getting help is not failing

Next: Chapter 3 - When Your Body Speaks

(Take at least a week with this chapter first)

CHAPTER 3 WORKBOOK

When Your Body Speaks: What Your Symptoms Might Be Saying

SPEAKING IT TRUE - The Monday Headache

Sunday night:

Your mind says: "Tomorrow will be fine"

Your body says: "Starting the headache early"

Your jaw says: "Clenching for the week ahead"

The truth: "My body is already responding to stress I haven't admitted yet"

Important: Physical symptoms have many causes. Always check with a doctor first.

This chapter explores ONE possible factor - how emotions sometimes show up in our bodies. This is about noticing patterns, not replacing medical care.

Welcome to Chapter 3

Your body might be trying to tell you something. Not in a mystical way - in a real, physical way.

Have you noticed:

☐ Headaches after certain phone calls?

☐ Stomach problems during stressful times?

☐ Back pain when you feel unsupported?

☐ Getting sick before things you dread?

☐ Your jaw hurting from clenching?

These connections are real. Stress creates actual physical changes in your body.

Quick Check: Your Body Map

Where does stress usually show up for you?

☐ Head (headaches, migraines)

☐ Jaw (clenching, TMJ, teeth grinding)

☐ Throat (tight, hard to swallow, losing voice)

☐ Shoulders (tight, up at ears, aching)

☐ Chest (tight, hard to breathe, heart racing)

☐ Stomach (upset, nauseous, IBS symptoms)

☐ Back (lower back pain, upper back tight)

Everyone's body speaks differently. There's no wrong answer.

Understanding the Connection

How stress becomes physical:

1. Something stressful happens (or might happen)

2. Your body releases stress chemicals

3. These chemicals cause real physical changes:

- Muscles tighten ($\rightarrow$ pain)
- Digestion changes ($\rightarrow$ stomach issues)
- Blood vessels constrict ($\rightarrow$ headaches)
- Inflammation increases ($\rightarrow$ various symptoms)

These aren't "in your head" - they're real physical responses.

This Week's Practice: The Body-Stress Detective

Day 1-2: Track the Pattern

Time	What Happened	Body Response
Morning		
Afternoon		
Evening		

Look for connections. No judgment - just curiosity.

SPEAKING IT TRUE - Your Body's Message

Fill in your pattern:

When _____ happens

My _____ starts hurting

My body might be saying: _____

What I couldn't say out loud: _____

Day 3-4: The Timeline Check

Think about your most common symptom. Now track backwards:

What happened 24-48 hours BEFORE the symptom?

Who were you with?

What couldn't you express?

Sometimes our bodies react to things before our minds catch up.

Common Body-Emotion Patterns

These are patterns some people notice. Yours might be different:

Jaw/Teeth: Often connected to anger we're holding back or words we're not saying

Shoulders: Might carry burdens, responsibilities, or bracing for impact

Stomach: Sometimes processes emotions we can't "digest" or accept

Back: May relate to feeling unsupported or carrying too much

Headaches: Can connect to overthinking or conflicting thoughts

Throat: Might tighten when we can't speak our truth

My pattern seems to be:

When I feel _____

My _____ reacts

Day 5-6: The Body Conversation

Try talking to your symptom (yes, really):

"Hey [body part], what are you trying to tell me?"

Write whatever comes to mind, even if it seems silly:

Working WITH Your Body

When you notice a symptom starting:

1. **Pause:** "My body is reacting to something"

2. **Check:** "What just happened? What am I feeling?"

3. **Acknowledge:** "Thank you, body, for the information"

4. **Express:** Say out loud (when alone) what you couldn't say

5. **Care:** Give your body what it needs (rest, movement, warmth)

Day 7: The Expression Experiment

This week, try ONE of these:

☐ When jaw clenches: Say the angry words (alone, in car)

☐ When stomach hurts: Journal what you can't "digest"

☐ When shoulders tighten: Name what you're carrying

☐ When head hurts: Write down all the spinning thoughts

☐ When back aches: Ask "Where do I need support?"

What happened when you tried it?

SPEAKING IT TRUE - Week's End

What you discovered:

My body has been: *"Holding what I couldn't express"*

The symptoms are: *"Real, even when the cause is emotional"*

When I listen: *"Sometimes the pain has information"*

My practice: *"Notice the connection, express what's stuck"*

The Stress-Symptom Tracker

Fill this out over the week:

Day	Stress Event	Body Response	What Helped
Mon			
Tue			
Wed			
Thu			
Fri			

Important Reminders

See a doctor if:

- Symptoms are new or getting worse
- Pain is severe or persistent
- You have other concerning symptoms
- Emotional work isn't helping physical symptoms

This work adds to medical care, never replaces it.

Your Body Wisdom Notes

This week I learned my body:

One pattern I noticed:

Something I want to remember:

Gentle Practices for Common Symptoms

For Tension Headaches:

- Notice jaw and shoulders

- Gentle neck rolls

- Cool cloth on forehead

- Express what's "stuck in your head"

For Stomach Issues:

- Breathe deeply into belly

- Journal what's hard to "digest"

- Warm compress

- Gentle movement

For Back Pain:

- Ask: "What am I carrying?"

- Gentle stretching

- Name where you need support

- Rest without guilt

Remember This Week

- Physical symptoms from stress are real

- Your body might be holding unexpressed emotions

- Listening to symptoms is different from fixing them

- Sometimes expressing the emotion helps the symptom

- Always check medical causes too

- Your body is trying to protect you, not punish you

- Small expressions can make big differences

Your Permission Note

I give myself permission to:

- Have physical responses to emotional stress

- Take my symptoms seriously

- Express what I've been holding back (safely, alone)

- Get medical help when needed

- Rest when my body asks

- Be curious instead of judgmental about symptoms

Signed: _____

Date: _____

Crisis Resources

If symptoms are overwhelming or you're in crisis:

- Call 988 (mental health crisis)
- Call 911 (medical emergency)
- Text HOME to 741741
- Contact your doctor

Next: Chapter 4 - Finding One Safe Place

(When your whole body feels activated)

CHAPTER 4 WORKBOOK

Finding One Safe Place: When Everything Feels Too Much

SPEAKING IT TRUE - The Body Storm

When panic hits:

Your chest says: "Can't breathe!"

Your stomach says: "Going to be sick!"

Your legs say: "RUN NOW!"

But your earlobe says: "...I'm just an earlobe. I'm fine."

The truth: "Not every part of me is in crisis."

Welcome to Chapter 4

This chapter is for when your whole body feels like a fire alarm going off. When every part feels wrong, tight, or screaming.

If you often feel:

☐ Everything in my body is wrong

☐ I can't find any comfortable position

☐ My whole body is one big panic

☐ There's nowhere safe in my own skin

☐ Body scans make things worse, not better

This chapter will help you find just ONE calm spot. That's all you need.

The Problem with "Just Relax"

People tell you to:

"Scan your body and relax each part" (but every part is screaming)

"Feel your feelings" (but they're too big)

"Be present in your body" (but your body feels dangerous)

> **The solution isn't relaxing your whole body. It's finding ONE boring, neutral spot that proves not everything is on fire.**

Your Safe Spot Search

Let's find your boring spot. Check any that feel neutral/calm/nothing special:

- [ ] Right earlobe
- [ ] Left earlobe
- [ ] Tip of nose
- [ ] One fingernail
- [ ] Pinky finger
- [ ] Elbow
- [ ] Knee
- [ ] Big toe
- [ ] Space between fingers
- [ ] Behind your ear

If none of these work, that's okay. Keep looking. Everyone has at least one boring spot.

Why One Neutral Spot Matters

Your neutral spot is proof that:

- Not every part of you is in crisis
- Your whole body isn't actually on fire
- There's at least one safe place in your skin
- The panic isn't everywhere (even when it feels like it)

This one spot becomes your anchor when everything else is chaos.

This Week's Practice: Building Your Anchor

Day 1-2: Finding Your Spot

Try this throughout the day:

Time	Body Part I Checked	Feels Neutral? (Y/N)
Morning		
Afternoon		
Evening		

My most neutral spot seems to be: _____

SPEAKING IT TRUE - Your Calm Spot

When I found my neutral spot:

My panic said: *"Everything is terrible!"*

My [neutral spot] said: _____

I realized: _____

This means: *"I have one place that's already okay"*

Day 3-4: Using Your Anchor

When you feel overwhelmed, try this:

1. Notice: "Everything feels bad right now"

2. Remember: "Except my [neutral spot]"

3. Touch or focus on that spot

4. Say: "This part is calm. I have one calm place."

5. Stay with it for 30 seconds

Track your practice:

☐ Used my anchor during stress

☐ Remembered it exists when panicking

☐ Touched it when overwhelmed

☐ Noticed it stayed calm when everything else wasn't

Day 5-6: Growing Awareness

Can you find a second neutral spot?

First neutral spot: _____

Second neutral spot (if found): _____

> **The Growing Calm Practice:**
>
> 1. Start with your first neutral spot
>
> 2. Notice it's calm
>
> 3. Check if the area next to it is also calm
>
> 4. Don't force it - just notice
>
> 5. Some days the calm spreads, some days it doesn't

Day 7: Integration

This week with my neutral spot:

Times I remembered to find it: _____

What it felt like to have one calm place:

One thing that surprised me:

Common Neutral Spots

People often find these spots are neutral (yours might be different):

Often Neutral:

- Earlobes (rarely hold tension)
- Elbows (just doing their job)
- Pinky fingers (often forgotten by stress)
- Knees (boring joints)
- The arch of your foot

Usually NOT Neutral:

- Chest (holds anxiety)
- Stomach (processes emotions)
- Shoulders (carry tension)
- Jaw (holds anger)
- Lower back (stores stress)

Your body is unique. Trust what you find, not what "should" be neutral.

When You Can't Find Any Neutral Spot

If everything feels activated:

☐ Try again tomorrow (capacity changes daily)

☐ Try right after waking (body often calmer)

☐ Try after a warm shower

☐ Try the space between body parts

☐ Try external anchors (smooth stone, soft fabric)

Some days are too activated. That's information, not failure.

SPEAKING IT TRUE - Week's End

What changed:

Beginning of week: *"My whole body is chaos"*

My discovery: *"My [spot] is actually fine"*

What this means: *"Not everything is emergency"*

My practice now: *"Find my anchor when overwhelmed"*

Emergency Anchor Plan

For panic moments, write your plan:

When I'm overwhelmed:

1. My neutral spot is: _____

2. I can find it by: _____

3. I'll touch/focus on it for: _____ seconds

4. I'll remind myself: _____

Building Your Toolkit

Other things that help when my whole body feels activated:

☐ Hold ice cube (strong sensation that's not panic)

☐ Splash cold water on face

☐ Press feet firmly into floor

☐ Hold something soft

☐ Count backwards from 100

☐ Name 5 things I can see

The Advanced Practice (Optional)

Only try this after finding your neutral spot reliably:

The Percentage Check:

When activated, ask:

- What percentage of me is panicking?

- What percentage is neutral/calm?

Example: "80% panic, 20% okay"

Sometimes just noticing that ANY percentage is calm helps.

Important Reminders

- You only need ONE neutral spot
- Boring is perfect - boring means not activated
- Your neutral spot might change day to day
- This isn't about relaxing everything
- It's about proving not everything is crisis
- Some days you won't find it - that's okay
- The practice is looking, not always finding

Your Permission Note

I give myself permission to:

- Have most of my body feel bad

- Only find one tiny calm spot

- Forget my neutral spot exists when panicking

- Take weeks to trust this practice

- Have days when I can't find any calm

- Count one neutral earlobe as success

Signed: _____

When to Seek Additional Help

Consider professional support if:

- You never feel safe in your body
- Panic attacks are frequent (multiple times per week)
- You're dissociating regularly (feeling outside your body)
- These practices increase your distress
- You're having thoughts of self-harm

This practice helps but isn't treatment for trauma or panic disorders.

Remember This Week

- One calm spot is enough
- Boring is the goal - boring means safe
- Your earlobe doesn't care about your problems
- Not everything in your body is activated (even when it feels like it)
- This one spot is your proof of safety
- Finding it is success, using it is bonus
- This builds slowly - be patient

Next: Chapter 5 - When Your Capacity Changes

Why some days everything's fine and others nothing is)

END OF PART ONE

• • •

You've built the foundation: awareness.

- You can notice patterns (sometimes)

- You found your observer

- You recognize protection

- You hear body signals

- You located one safe spot

Even if you only experienced these briefly,
you have enough to continue.

• • •

*Continue to Part Two when ready to
experiment with what you notice.*

There's no rush.

Stay with Part One as long as needed.

PART TWO

Learning to Move

Practical experiments for different body states

Notice first—
the shoulders climbing,
the breath holding,
the pattern running.

Validate second—
"This makes sense because..."
"My body learned this when..."
"It's trying to protect me from..."

Only then, the tiniest adjustment—
one breath deeper,
shoulders dropping half an inch,
feet finding floor.

Skip to step three,
and the body rebels.
"You don't understand the danger!"
it screams, getting louder.

But acknowledge first?
"I see you. I hear you. You make sense"—
and sometimes, just sometimes,
the body softens enough to try.

What Changes in Part Two

Part One taught you to notice. Now comes the question that probably brought you to this book: *What do I actually DO when I notice?*

You can observe yourself checking locks five times, but how do you stop at three? You notice your capacity is limited today, but how do you actually work with that? You recognize anxiety rising, but then what?

This is where most approaches fail. They jump straight to techniques—breathe deeply, think positively, just relax—without acknowledging what your body is experiencing.

Your nervous system rejects help it hasn't asked for.

THE THREE-STEP PATTERN

Every technique in Part Two follows this sequence:

1. **NOTICE (from Part One):** "My shoulders are at my ears."

2. **VALIDATE (new):** "This makes sense because I'm about to see my mother who always criticizes me."

3. **TINY ADJUSTMENT (new):** "Let me drop them half an inch. Not relaxed, just slightly less armored."

Skip validation and the adjustment rarely works.

Your body rebels against change it hasn't agreed to.

Why This Pattern Works

For years, I tried breathing exercises for anxiety. They made it worse. My body would tighten more, as if fighting the forced calm.

Then a somatic therapist taught me to acknowledge first: "I'm anxious about tomorrow's presentation, and that makes complete sense because the stakes are real."

Same breathing technique. Completely different result.

The acknowledgment changed everything. My body felt heard. It stopped fighting. The breathing actually helped.

This is Part Two's foundation: *Your body needs to be heard before it will listen.*

• • •

Your Journey Through Part Two

Chapter 5: When Your Capacity Changes

Your awareness from Part One lets you recognize window days (lots of capacity) versus keyhole days (minimal capacity). Now you'll learn to adjust accordingly—scaling your actions to match your actual capacity rather than forcing yourself through.

Practice focus: Honoring capacity changes

Chapter 6: When Anxiety Makes Sense

Using your observer capacity, you can now notice when anxiety carries accurate information versus old patterns. This awareness lets you choose your response—when to take action versus when to soothe.

Practice focus: Distinguishing anxiety types

Chapter 7: When Sleep Won't Come

Your neutral zone from Chapter 4 becomes your anchor when your night guard won't stand down. You'll learn to acknowledge your guard's vigilance, then guide attention to your neutral spot.

Practice focus: Working with sleep resistance

Chapter 8: Movement as Medicine

All of Part One's awareness culminates here: recognizing your patterns lets you accurately identify what movement medicine your body needs. Different states need different movement.

Practice focus: Matching movement to nervous system state

● ● ●

Managing Expectations

Some days these practices will help. Your anxiety might soften after acknowledgment. You might sleep after thanking your night guard. Movement might discharge the activation.

Other days, nothing helps. You'll notice, validate, try to adjust, and the pattern runs anyway.

This isn't failure—it's information about your nervous system's current state.

• • •

How to Work with Part Two Exercises

Remember: Validation is the KEY

When you notice a pattern, resist the urge to immediately try to change it. Instead:

1. **First, really notice:** Where is it in your body? How intense? What triggered it?

2. **Second, validate thoroughly:**

    "This makes sense because..."

    "My body is trying to protect me from..."

    "I learned this was necessary when..."

    "Given my history/current stress/exhaustion, of course this is happening"

3. **Third, try the TINIEST adjustment:**

    Not from tense to relaxed, but tense to slightly less tense

    Not from panic to calm, but panic to panic-with-awareness

    Not from yes to no, but yes to "let me think about it"

When NOT to Push

Don't force adjustments when:

- You're in crisis (prioritize safety)
- You're completely depleted (rest is the adjustment)
- The pattern is protecting you from real, current danger
- Your body strongly rejects even tiny changes

Sometimes validation alone is enough. The body just needed to be heard.

What "Success" Looks Like in Part Two

Success IS:

- *Remembering to validate before trying to change*
- *Making a 1% adjustment instead of forcing 100% change*
- *Noticing when practices help AND when they don't*
- *Staying conscious while patterns run*
- *Being kind when nothing works*

Success IS NOT:

- *Patterns stopping completely*
- *Perfect calm or regulation*
- *Techniques working every time*
- *Feeling "fixed" or "healed"*

Before You Begin Part Two

Take a moment to appreciate what you built in Part One. You now have:

- Observer capacity to notice patterns
- Understanding of protection versus self-sabotage
- Awareness of body signals
- At least one neutral anchor point

These aren't small achievements. They're the foundation that makes Part Two's experiments possible.

Part Two Key Principle:

Awareness comes first.
Validation before regulation.
Tiny movements, not forcing.

Some days you can adjust.
Some days you can only notice.
Some days surviving is enough.

You'll forget this pattern.
You'll remember again.
That's the practice.

Turn the page to begin Chapter 5:
When Your Capacity Changes Your first experiment in working WITH your
nervous system's reality rather than against it.

CHAPTER 5 WORKBOOK

When Your Capacity Changes: Why Yesterday's Normal Is Today's Impossible

SPEAKING IT TRUE - The Capacity Mystery

Yesterday:

Me: "I can handle anything! Bring it on!"

My capacity: Wide open window

Today:

Me: "A text notification just made me cry"

My capacity: Tiny keyhole

The truth: "Same person, different capacity. Both are real."

Welcome to Chapter 5

Ever wonder why some days you can handle everything and other days a doorbell destroys you?

This chapter explains:

- Why your capacity changes daily (sometimes hourly)

- What "window" vs "keyhole" days mean

- How to honor your actual capacity instead of forcing through

- Why this isn't weakness - it's biology

Quick Capacity Check

Right now, today, which feels more true?

WINDOW DAY (Wide Capacity)

- [ ] I can handle complexity
- [ ] Noise is fine
- [ ] People are manageable
- [ ] Problems feel solvable
- [ ] I have energy for others

KEYHOLE DAY (Minimal Capacity)

- [ ] Everything is too much
- [ ] Sounds hurt
- [ ] Can't people
- [ ] Tiny tasks feel huge
- [ ] No energy for anything

Today feels like: [ ] **Window** [ ] **Keyhole** [ ] **Somewhere Between**

What Affects Your Capacity

Check what impacted your capacity this week:

- [ ] Sleep quality (one bad night = 30% less capacity)
- [ ] Stress accumulation (it adds up)
- [ ] Social interactions (draining or energizing?)
- [ ] Work demands
- [ ] Family stuff
- [ ] Health/hormones/pain
- [ ] Weather changes
- [ ] Anniversary reactions (body remembers dates)
- [ ] News/world events
- [ ] No idea but capacity is different

This Week's Capacity Tracking

Track your window/keyhole patterns to understand YOUR rhythm:

Day	Morning Capacity	Afternoon Capacity	Evening Capacity	What Affected It?
Monday	☐ W ☐ K	☐ W ☐ K	☐ W ☐ K	
Tuesday	☐ W ☐ K	☐ W ☐ K	☐ W ☐ K	
Wednesday	☐ W ☐ K	☐ W ☐ K	☐ W ☐ K	
Thursday	☐ W ☐ K	☐ W ☐ K	☐ W ☐ K	
Friday	☐ W ☐ K	☐ W ☐ K	☐ W ☐ K	
Saturday	☐ W ☐ K	☐ W ☐ K	☐ W ☐ K	
Sunday	☐ W ☐ K	☐ W ☐ K	☐ W ☐ K	

W = Window (wide capacity), K = Keyhole (minimal capacity)

SPEAKING IT TRUE - The Capacity Conversation

Them: *"Can you help me move this weekend?"*

Your mouth (on a window day): *"Sure! Happy to!"*

Your mouth (on a keyhole day): *"Sure! Happy to!"*

Your body (on a keyhole day): *"NOOOOOO! We have nothing left!"*

The practice: *"Let me check my capacity and get back to you."*

Honoring Window Days

When you have wide capacity, use it wisely:

DO:

☐ Schedule challenging conversations

☐ Take on complex projects

☐ Offer support to others

☐ Try new things

☐ Handle difficult tasks

DON'T:

☐ Use ALL your capacity (save 20%)

☐ Commit future keyhole days

☐ Assume tomorrow will be the same

Surviving Keyhole Days

When capacity is minimal:

CANCEL OR POSTPONE:

☐ Non-essential meetings

☐ Social obligations

☐ Emotionally demanding tasks

☐ Anything that can wait

FOCUS ON:

☐ Absolute essentials only

☐ Basic self-care

☐ Saying "no" or "not today"

☐ Resting without guilt

Remember: Keyhole days are not character flaws. They're nervous system reality.

The Capacity Debt Tracker

When you use all your window-day capacity, you create "capacity debt" – expect keyhole days after.

This week's capacity spending:

Big event/stress on: _____

Capacity crash happened: _____ days later

Recovery took: _____ days

Most people need 1-3 recovery days after major capacity use.

Creating Your Capacity Communication Plan

Practice phrases for different capacity states:

For Window Days:

"I have capacity today. What do you need?"

"I can help with that."

"Let me take that on."

For Keyhole Days:

"I'm having a limited capacity day."

"I can't take on anything extra today."

"Let me get back to you when I have more bandwidth."

"I need to protect my energy today."

For Uncertain Days:

"Let me check my capacity and get back to you."

"I need to see how I feel tomorrow."

"Can I let you know in the morning?"

Your Personal Capacity Patterns

After tracking this week, what did you notice?

I tend to have MORE capacity:

I tend to have LESS capacity:

My capacity crashes most predictably after:

SPEAKING IT TRUE - The Permission Slip

Society says: *"Push through! Mind over matter!"*

Your keyhole day says: *"I literally cannot."*

The truth: *"Honoring low capacity takes more wisdom than forcing through."*

Permission granted: *"I can cancel, rest, say no, and protect my limited resources."*

Planning Around Capacity Changes

Look at next week. Plan for capacity reality:

Day	Predicted Capacity	Scheduled Demands	Adjustment Needed?
Monday			
Tuesday			
Wednesday			
Thursday			
Friday			

If you have a big event, schedule recovery time after!

Emergency Keyhole Day Plan

For sudden capacity crashes, have this ready:

People I can text "Having a keyhole day":

1. _____

2. _____

Things I can cancel without major consequences:

1. _____

2. _____

3. _____

Bare minimum that must happen:

1. _____

2. _____

My keyhole day self-care:

☐ Order takeout (no cooking)

☐ Cancel everything possible

☐ Go to bed early

☐ No guilt allowed

The Both/And Practice

Practice holding both truths:

- I am capable AND I have limited capacity today

- I want to help AND I need to protect my energy

- I care about others AND I must care for myself

- Yesterday I could AND today I cannot

Both can be true. Capacity changes don't change your worth.

Common Capacity Questions

Q: "Why can I handle crisis but not normal days?"

A: Crisis mobilizes all reserves. You're borrowing from tomorrow. The crash comes later.

Q: "Why are mornings different from evenings?"

A: Capacity depletes throughout the day. Most people start higher, end lower.

Q: "Is it okay to have keyhole WEEKS?"

A: Yes. Chronic stress, illness, or major life changes can create extended low capacity. This is information, not failure.

Weekly Reflection

After tracking capacity this week:

Number of window days: _____

Number of keyhole days: _____

Number of mixed days: _____

What I learned about my patterns:

How I honored (or didn't honor) my capacity:

One thing I'll do differently next week:

Building Capacity Slowly

If you're stuck in chronic keyhole mode:

- [ ] Start with micro-increases (5% more, not 50%)
- [ ] Protect sleep fiercely
- [ ] Say no to energy drains
- [ ] Add one tiny pleasant thing daily
- [ ] Track what gives vs. takes energy
- [ ] Consider professional support

Building capacity is like physical therapy - slow, steady, patient.

Your Capacity Bill of Rights

I have the right to:

- Have different capacity than yesterday

- Cancel when I'm depleted

- Protect my energy

- Rest without earning it

- Say "I don't have capacity for that"

- Take recovery time after big events

- Have keyhole days without shame

- Honor my actual limits

Signed: _____

Date: _____

Remember This Week

- Capacity changes are NORMAL, not character flaws

- Window and keyhole days both have purpose

- Using all capacity creates debt (expect crashes)

- Honoring limits prevents bigger crashes

- Communication about capacity helps everyone

- Rest is not laziness when capacity is low

- Tomorrow's capacity might be completely different

End of Chapter 5 Workbook

Next: Chapter 6 - When Anxiety Makes Sense

(Sometimes your body is right to be alarmed)

CHAPTER 6 WORKBOOK

When Anxiety Makes Sense: Sometimes Your Body Is Right to Be Alarmed

SPEAKING IT TRUE - Anxiety's Messages

Your anxiety says: *"DANGER! THREAT! PROBLEM!"*

Your mind says: *"Stop overreacting!"*

But sometimes: *Your anxiety is right*

The truth: *"Anxiety isn't the enemy. It's information that needs translation."*

Welcome to Chapter 6

Anxiety isn't always wrong. Sometimes it's giving you accurate information about real threats. Sometimes it's replaying old dangers. Sometimes you're just exhausted.

This chapter helps you distinguish:

• Accurate anxiety (current threat needing action)
• Historical anxiety (old threat replaying)
• Capacity anxiety (depleted and everything feels dangerous)

Quick Anxiety Assessment

Think of something making you anxious right now. Where do you feel it?

☐ **Gut (specific)** - Often accurate anxiety about real issue

☐ **Chest (tight)** - Often emotional/historical anxiety

☐ **Whole body (diffuse)** - Often capacity/depletion anxiety

☐ **Head (racing thoughts)** - Often trying to control outcome

☐ **Throat (closed)** - Often about speaking up/expression

☐ **Stomach (nausea)** - Often about digesting difficult situation

Body location is one clue, not definitive proof. Use it as information to explore further.

The Three Types of Anxiety

1. ACCURATE ANXIETY (Green Flag)

Your body is right - there's a real current threat:

☐ Someone repeatedly violates your boundaries

☐ A situation genuinely isn't safe

☐ Your values are being compromised

☐ Something needs to change

☐ You're unprepared for something important

Response needed: Take protective action

2. HISTORICAL ANXIETY (Yellow Flag)

Your body is time-traveling to old danger:

- ☐ Familiar feeling from childhood
- ☐ Reaction bigger than situation warrants
- ☐ Pattern repeats across different situations
- ☐ Can't articulate specific current threat
- ☐ Someone reminds you of someone else

Response needed: Soothe and ground in present

3. CAPACITY ANXIETY (Blue Flag)

Your body is depleted and everything feels threatening:

- ☐ Started after poor sleep/stress
- ☐ Everything feels equally dangerous
- ☐ Can't prioritize actual threats
- ☐ Worse when hungry/tired
- ☐ It's a keyhole day (Chapter 5)

Response needed: Rest and restore capacity

This Week's Anxiety Tracking

Track your anxiety patterns to understand what kind of information your body gives you:

Day	What Triggered Anxiety	Where I Felt It	Type (A/H/C)	What Helped
Monday				
Tuesday				
Wednesday				
Thursday				
Friday				
Saturday				
Sunday				

A = Accurate, H = Historical, C = Capacity

SPEAKING IT TRUE - The Anxiety Conversation

Old way:

Anxiety: *"PANIC!"*

You: *"Shut up! Stop overreacting!"*

Anxiety: *"PANIC LOUDER!"*

New way:

Anxiety: *"PANIC!"*

You: *"What are you trying to tell me?"*

Anxiety: *"This situation is like when..."*

You: *"Ah, I see. Thank you. Let me check if that's true now."*

Working with Accurate Anxiety

When anxiety is giving you real information about current threats:

Step 1: Thank It

"Thank you, anxiety, for alerting me to this real issue."

Step 2: Take Action

- ☐ Set the boundary that needs setting
- ☐ Have the difficult conversation
- ☐ Make the necessary change
- ☐ Prepare for the challenge
- ☐ Leave the unsafe situation

Step 3: Discharge the Energy

After taking action, your body still holds the activation:

- ☐ Shake it out (literally shake your body)
- ☐ Walk around the block
- ☐ Do 10 jumping jacks
- ☐ Take 5 deep breaths

Current threat I need to address: _____

Action I will take: _____

Working with Historical Anxiety

When anxiety is replaying old threats:

Step 1: Recognize the Time Travel

"My body is remembering old danger."

Step 2: Ground in Present

- ☐ Find your neutral spot (Chapter 4)
- ☐ Name 5 things you can see right now
- ☐ Feel your feet on the floor
- ☐ State current facts: "I'm [age], not [childhood age]"
- ☐ "This is [current person], not [past person]"

Step 3: Soothe the Activation

- ☐ Slow, gentle movement (not intense)
- ☐ Warm bath or shower
- ☐ Gentle touch (hand on heart)
- ☐ Quiet, safe environment

This anxiety reminds me of: _____

How old I feel when this happens: _____

What's different now: _____

Working with Capacity Anxiety

When anxiety is from depletion:

Step 1: Recognize Depletion

"This anxiety is telling me I'm out of capacity."

Step 2: Stop Trying to Figure It Out

When depleted, you can't accurately assess threats. Don't make big decisions.

Step 3: Rest and Restore

☐ Cancel non-essentials

☐ Eat something nourishing

☐ Sleep or rest

☐ Gentle restoration (not fixing)

☐ Wait 24 hours before big decisions

Signs I'm depleted: _____

What depleted me: _____

What restores me: _____

The Mixed Reality (Most Common)

Usually anxiety has multiple causes:

Example: Work presentation anxiety

- **Accurate part:** I am underprepared (need to prepare more)

- **Historical part:** Visibility meant criticism in my family

- **Capacity part:** I'm exhausted and everything feels harder

Response: Address ALL parts

- Prepare for presentation (accurate)

- Remind myself this isn't family (historical)

- Get good sleep before (capacity)

SPEAKING IT TRUE - The 24-Hour Rule

3 AM anxiety says: *"Everything is terrible! We must act NOW!"*

3 PM you says: *"Actually, that wasn't as bad as it seemed at 3 AM"*

The truth: *"Anxiety at 3 AM is usually 90% depletion, 10% reality"*

The practice: *"Wait 24 hours when unsure. Real threats stay real. Phantom threats often fade."*

Your Anxiety Response Plan

When anxiety arises, I will:

1. PAUSE AND ASK:

• Where do I feel this in my body? _____

• What triggered it? _____

• Does this feel familiar? _____

2. ASSESS TYPE:

☐ Accurate - real current threat

☐ Historical - old pattern activated

☐ Capacity - I'm depleted

☐ Mixed - combination

☐ Unsure - use 24-hour rule

3. RESPOND ACCORDINGLY:

My typical response will be: _____

Common Anxiety Patterns

Check which patterns you recognize:

☐ **Sunday Scaries:** Often capacity anxiety about the week ahead

☐ **3 AM Catastrophizing:** Almost always depletion anxiety

☐ **Before Social Events:** Often historical (past rejection/judgment)

☐ **Money Anxiety:** Can be accurate, historical, or both

☐ **Health Anxiety:** Mix of accurate concern and historical fear

☐ **Relationship Anxiety:** Often historical patterns in current situation

☐ **Work Performance:** Mix of all three types

The Anxiety Translator Practice

Practice translating anxiety into information:

Anxiety Says	Translation Might Be
"Everyone hates me!"	"I'm depleted and need rest" OR "That interaction was awkward"
"I'll be fired!"	"I need to prepare better" OR "Old perfectionism activated"
"Something bad will happen!"	"I'm exhausted" OR "This reminds me of when..."
_____	_____
_____	_____

Building Your Anxiety Toolkit

For Accurate Anxiety, I need:

- Courage to take action

- Support from: _____

- My action steps ready

- Way to discharge after: _____

For Historical Anxiety, I need:

- Grounding techniques that work for me: _____

- Reminders of present reality

- Soothing practices: _____

- Patience with the process

For Capacity Anxiety, I need:

- Permission to rest

- Quick nourishment options: _____

- Sleep protection strategies

- Things I can cancel: _____

Weekly Reflection

After tracking anxiety this week:

Most of my anxiety was: ☐ Accurate ☐ Historical ☐ Capacity ☐ Mixed

Patterns I noticed:

What helped most:

What I want to remember:

Important Reminders

- **Anxiety isn't your enemy** - it's your alarm system
- **Sometimes anxiety is right** - honor accurate warnings
- **Fighting anxiety makes it louder** - listening helps
- **The 24-hour rule works** - real threats stay real
- **Depletion anxiety lies** - don't trust 3 AM thoughts
- **Mixed anxiety is normal** - address all parts
- **You're learning anxiety's language** - be patient

When to Seek Support

Consider professional help if:

- Anxiety prevents daily functioning
- You can't distinguish between types after trying
- Panic attacks are frequent (multiple per week)
- Anxiety leads to substance use for coping
- You avoid necessary activities due to anxiety
- Physical symptoms are severe (can't breathe, chest pain)

These practices complement but don't replace professional treatment for anxiety disorders.

Your Anxiety Bill of Rights

I have the right to:

- Feel anxious without shame

- Take anxiety seriously as information

- Need time to assess what kind it is

- Take protective action when needed

- Rest when depleted

- Ask for help figuring it out

- Have mixed or unclear anxiety

- Get professional support

Signed: _____

Date: _____

End of Chapter 6 Workbook

Next: Chapter 7 - When Sleep Won't Come

(Your night guard and why it won't stand down)

CHAPTER 7 WORKBOOK

When Sleep Won't Come: Your Night Guard Won't Rest Until It Believes You're Safe

SPEAKING IT TRUE - The 3 AM Conversation

Your exhausted body: *"Please, we need to sleep"*

Your night guard: *"Absolutely not! Did you hear that sound?"*

Your body: *"That was the refrigerator"*

Your guard: *"But what if it wasn't? I must stay alert!"*

The truth: *"My guard is trying to protect me. It just needs to know we're safe."*

Welcome to Chapter 7

Your insomnia isn't random. Part of you—your "night guard"—won't let you become unconscious because it doesn't believe you're safe enough to power down.

This chapter helps you:

- Understand your night guard's job
- Identify what it's protecting you from
- Dialogue with it instead of fighting it
- Create conditions where it feels safe to rest

The goal isn't to eliminate your guard - it's to help it trust that rest is safe.

Meet Your Night Guard

Which type of night guard do you have? (Check all that apply)

THE SCANNER

- [ ] Monitors every sound in the house
- [ ] Checks the time repeatedly
- [ ] Reviews if doors are locked (mentally or physically)
- [ ] Listens for family members
- [ ] Can't rest until everyone else is safe

Often develops: In parents, caregivers, or after break-ins

THE REPLAYER

- [ ] Reviews today's conversations on loop
- [ ] Analyzes what you said/did wrong
- [ ] Replays embarrassing moments
- [ ] Can't let go of unfinished interactions
- [ ] Processes social threats

Often develops: With social anxiety or perfectionism

THE REHEARSER

- ☐ Plans tomorrow's conversations
- ☐ Imagines worst-case scenarios
- ☐ Prepares defenses and responses
- ☐ Creates to-do lists mentally
- ☐ Tries to control future outcomes

Often develops: During high-stress periods or transitions

THE PROCESSOR

- ☐ Solves work problems at 2 AM
- ☐ Analyzes everything that happened
- ☐ Creates elaborate plans
- ☐ Can't turn off the thinking
- ☐ Believes rest is wasted time

Often develops: In people with high responsibility

This Week's Sleep Tracking

Track your guard's concerns to understand what it's protecting:

Night	Time Awake	Guard Type Active	What It Worried About	What Helped (If Anything)
Monday				
Tuesday				
Wednesday				
Thursday				
Friday				
Saturday				
Sunday				

SPEAKING IT TRUE - The Guard Dialogue

Old way:

You: *"JUST LET ME SLEEP!"*

Guard: *"NO! DANGER!"*

You: *"THERE'S NO DANGER!"*

Guard: *"THAT'S WHAT YOU THINK!"*

New way:

You: *"Thank you for protecting me. What are you worried about?"*

Guard: *"What if [specific worry]?"*

You: *"I understand. Here's what's true right now..."*

Guard: *"Oh. Maybe we can rest a little."*

The Three-Step Sleep Practice

Step 1: NOTICE

"I'm awake at _____ AM"

"My guard is active - it's [scanning/replaying/rehearsing/processing]"

"My body is tired but activated"

Step 2: VALIDATE

"This makes sense because..."

- [ ] I'm stressed about tomorrow
- [ ] Something feels unfinished
- [ ] I'm responsible for others
- [ ] My nervous system learned nighttime isn't safe
- [ ] I'm in a new/unfamiliar placen

Step 3: ADJUST (Movement toward rest)

- [ ] Thank the guard for its service
- [ ] Provide current reality update
- [ ] Use physical movements to signal safety
- [ ] Accept whatever rest is possible

Dialogue with Your Night Guard

Tonight, try this conversation:

You: "Thank you for trying to keep me safe. What are you worried about?"

Guard might say: _____

You: "That makes sense because " _____

You: "Here's what's different now: " _____

You: "What would you need to feel safe enough to rest?"

Guard might need: _____

Physical Movements for Sleep

These movements signal safety to your nervous system:

For SCANNER Guards - The Safety Inventory

☐ Walk through house once (not repeatedly)

☐ Confirm doors locked (once)

☐ Check loved ones are safe (one text)

☐ Touch your neutral spot (Chapter 4)

☐ Say aloud: "Everyone is safe right now"

For REPLAYER Guards - The Discharge Shake

- [ ] Stand beside bed
- [ ] Gently shake whole body for 30 seconds
- [ ] Let jaw go loose
- [ ] Imagine shaking off the day
- [ ] Return to bed with "clean slate"

For REHEARSER Guards - The Progressive Settlement

vStart standing, take 3 breaths

- [ ] Sit on bed edge, 3 more breaths
- [ ] Lie down, 3 final breaths
- [ ] Each position signals moving toward rest
- [ ] Tell guard: "Tomorrow will handle itself"

For PROCESSOR Guards - The Butterfly Hug

- [ ] Cross arms over chest
- [ ] Alternately tap shoulders
- [ ] Continue for 1-2 minutes
- [ ] Helps integrate the day's processing
- [ ] Signals "processing complete"

Creating Safety Signals

Your nervous system needs consistent cues that rest is safe:

Environmental Safety

My guard feels safer when:

Door is:	☐ Open	☐ Closed	☐ Cracked
Light is:	☐ On	☐ Off	☐ Night light
Phone is:	☐ Visible	☐ Away	☐ On silent
I sleep:	☐ Back to wall	☐ Facing door	☐ Other
Covers are:	☐ Weighted	☐ Light	☐ Tucked

Other things that help: _____

SPEAKING IT TRUE - The Paradox

The pressure: *"I MUST sleep or tomorrow is ruined!"*

The guard: *"Pressure means danger! Stay alert!"*

The paradox: *"Accepting I might not sleep makes sleep more likely"*

The practice: *"I'll rest my body even if my mind stays active"*

The Paradoxical Approach

Sometimes accepting wakefulness helps more than forcing sleep:

Instead of: "I have to sleep NOW!"

Try: "I might not sleep tonight, and I'll survive"

Instead of: "This is a disaster!"

Try: "One bad night won't ruin everything"

Instead of: Fighting the guard

Try: "Thank you for your vigilance. I'll rest while you keep watch"

Your Bedtime Ritual

Create a consistent sequence that signals safety:

30 minutes before bed:

1. _____

2. _____

10 minutes before:

3. _____

4. _____

In bed:

5. Thank guard: "Thank you for _____ "

6. Reality check: "Right now we are _____ "

7. Permission: "You can rest or stay alert, either is okay"

When Sleep Anxiety Makes It Worse

The vicious cycle:

Can't sleep → Worry about not sleeping → More activated → Less able to sleep

Breaking the cycle:

☐ Acknowledge: "I'm anxious about sleep itself"

☐ Validate: "This makes sense - sleep has been hard"

☐ Adjust: "Rest is valuable even without sleep"

☐ Accept: "My guard is doing its best"

Emergency Middle-of-Night Plan

When I wake at 3 AM, I will:

1. Check time only once

2. Say: "Hello, guard. What's up?"

3. Listen for the worry

4. If worry is about tomorrow: Write it down, say "Tomorrow will handle this"

5. If worry is scanning: Do one safety check, say "All is well"

6. If can't return to sleep in 20 minutes: Get up, do quiet activity

7. Return to bed only when sleepy

Weekly Reflection

After tracking sleep this week:

My guard is most active when: _____

It's usually worried about: _____

What helped most: _____

Patterns I noticed:

What my guard might need to hear:

Important Reminders

- **Your night guard isn't the enemy** - it's trying to protect you

- **Fighting increases activation** - dialogue works better

- **Some nights the guard won't rest** - that's information, not failure

- **Accepting wakefulness paradoxically helps**

- **Rest has value even without sleep**

- **Your guard developed for good reasons**

- **Trust builds slowly** - be patient

When to Seek Support

Consider professional help if:

- Insomnia persists beyond 3 months (chronic insomnia)

- Sleep problems occur 3+ nights per week

- You're using alcohol/substances to sleep

- Daytime functioning is severely impaired

- You have signs of sleep apnea (gasping, snoring)

- Insomnia is accompanied by severe depression/anxiety

- You're having thoughts of self-harm from exhaustion

These practices complement but don't replace medical evaluation for sleep disorders.

Your Sleep Bill of Rights

I have the right to:

• Have a vigilant night guard

• Not sleep perfectly every night

• Rest even if I can't sleep

• Take time to feel safe

• Thank my guard for protecting me

• Need different conditions than others

• Seek help if needed

• Trust this process slowly

Signed: _____

Date: _____

End of Chapter 7 Workbook

Next: Chapter 8 - Movement as Medicine

(Different nervous system states need different movement)

CHAPTER 8 WORKBOOK

Movement as Medicine: Why Your Body Needs Different Movement on Different Days

SPEAKING IT TRUE - The Body's Request

Yesterday's body: *"Run! Move! I need to discharge this energy!"*

Today's body: *"Please no. Even walking feels impossible."*

Society: *"Just exercise! It helps everything!"*

The truth: *"Same movement that helps when resourced can harm when depleted."*

Welcome to Chapter 8

Exercise isn't one-size-fits-all medicine. Your nervous system needs different types of movement depending on its current state.

This chapter helps you:

• Recognize your current movement needs
• Match movement to your nervous system state
• Know when rest IS the medicine
• Understand when exercise helps vs. harms

The goal isn't to exercise more - it's to move in ways that actually serve your current state.

Quick Body State Check

Right now, which best describes how your body feels?

ACTIVATED/OVERFLOWING

- [ ] Can't sit still
- [ ] Vibrating with energy
- [ ] Racing thoughts
- [ ] Jaw clenching
- [ ] Feel like I'll explode without outlet

Needs: Discharge through vigorous movement

EXHAUSTED/DEPLETED

- [ ] Body feels impossibly heavy
- [ ] Everything requires enormous effort
- [ ] Been pushing through for days
- [ ] "Tired but wired" feeling
- [ ] Can barely find neutral spot (Ch. 4)

Needs: Gentle movement or complete rest

THE REHEARSER

- ☐ Feel outside my body
- ☐ World seems unreal
- ☐ Can't feel sensations clearly
- ☐ Going through motions automatically
- ☐ Numb or spacey

Needs: Grounding movement that enhances body awareness

THE PROCESSOR

- ☐ Can tune into body preferences
- ☐ Movement feels optional, not compulsive
- ☐ Can rest without guilt
- ☐ Body signals are clear
- ☐ Have genuine choice

Needs: Whatever feels good; time to build capacity

This Week's Movement Tracking

Track which movement helps or harms based on your state:

Day	Body State	Movement I Did	How It Felt	What I Needed
Monday				
Tuesday				
Wednesday				
Thursday				
Friday				
Saturday				
Sunday				

States: A = Activated, E = Exhausted, D = Disconnected, B = Balanced

SPEAKING IT TRUE - The Movement Mismatch

Exhausted body: *"I can't move"*

Advice: *"Push through! No pain, no gain!"*

Result: *Injury, deeper exhaustion, system crash*

Activated body: *"I need to RUN!"*

Advice: *"Try gentle yoga to calm down"*

Result: *More agitation, feeling trapped*

The truth: *"Match the medicine to the state"*

Movement for ACTIVATED States

When you need to discharge energy:

DO THIS:

- [ ] Running or sprints
- [ ] Jumping jacks (start with 10)
- [ ] Dancing vigorously
- [ ] Punching bag/shadow boxing
- [ ] Whole body shaking
- [ ] Cold shower after

AVOID:

- [ ] Forced stillness
- [ ] Slow gentle yoga (too frustrating)
- [ ] Meditation (impossible when activated)

Duration: Until you feel the edge come off (usually 10-20 minutes)

My go-to activated discharge: _____

Movement for EXHAUSTED States

When you're completely depleted:

DO THIS:

- [ ] Walk to mailbox (tiny movement)
- [ ] Gentle stretching in bed
- [ ] Sitting outside (movement to fresh air)
- [ ] One single yoga pose
- [ ] Permission to rest completely

AVOID:

- [ ] High intensity anything
- [ ] "Pushing through"
- [ ] Comparing to yesterday's capacity

Remember: Rest IS medicine when exhausted

My smallest possible movement: _____

Permission I need to rest: _____

Movement for DISCONNECTED States

When you feel outside your body:

DO THIS:

- [ ] Press feet firmly into floor
- [ ] Hold ice or textured objects
- [ ] Balance exercises
- [ ] Walking while counting steps
- [ ] Swimming (water provides boundaries)
- [ ] Yoga with focus on sensation

AVOID:

- [ ] Cardio that increases floating
- [ ] Movement without awareness

Duration: Until you feel the edge come off (usually 10-20 minutes)

My go-to activated discharge: _____

Movement for BALANCED States

When you have genuine choice:

THIS IS THE TIME TO:

- [ ] Try new activities

- [ ] Build capacity gradually

- [ ] Exercise for enjoyment

- [ ] Social movement (sports, classes)

- [ ] Progressive challenges

- [ ] Or rest if that's what calls

This is when standard exercise recommendations (150 min/week) work well!

Movement I enjoy when resourced: _____

How I want to build capacity: _____

SPEAKING IT TRUE - When Movement Harms

The pressure: *"I should exercise to feel better"*

The reality: *Forces intense workout while exhausted*

The result: *Injury, deeper depletion, self-blame*

The truth: *"Sometimes NOT exercising is self-care"*

When Exercise Makes Things WORSE

Exercise can harm when:

☐ You're deeply exhausted (keyhole days)

☐ It triggers panic attacks

☐ You're forcing it out of shame

☐ It's becoming compulsive

☐ You're ignoring pain signals

☐ It's late evening (disrupts sleep)

Trust your body over any "should" about exercise

The Three-Step Movement Practice

Before any movement:

Step 1: NOTICE

"My body feels _____ "

"My energy is _____ "

"I'm in a _____ state"

Step 2: VALIDATE

"This makes sense because _____ "

"My body needs _____ "

Step 3: ADJUST

"Today's movement medicine is _____ "

"Or rest if that's what's needed"

Building Your Movement Toolkit

For activated days, I have:

• Safe discharge option: _____

• Where I can do it: _____

• How long helps: _____

For exhausted days, I have:

• Tiniest movement: _____

• Permission to rest from: _____

• Gentle option: _____

For disconnected days, I have:

• Grounding movement: _____

• What brings me back: _____

For balanced days, I enjoy:

• Fun movement: _____

• Social option: _____

• New challenge: _____

Progressive Challenge (When Ready)

Building capacity gradually:

Week 1: Current comfortable level

Week 2: Add 5-10% more (time or intensity)

Week 3: Maintain or add another 5%

Week 4: Rest week (reduce by 25%)

Only progress when in balanced/resourced state!

My starting point: _____

My first tiny increase: _____

The Both/And Reality

Hold these truths together:

• I know exercise helps AND I can't do it today

• I need movement AND I need rest

• I want to be active AND my body says no

• Yesterday I could AND today I cannot

This isn't failure. It's information about current capacity.

Weekly Reflection

After tracking movement this week:

States I was in most: _____

Movement that helped: _____

Movement that didn't: _____

What surprised me:

What I want to remember:

Important Reminders

- **Standard recommendations work when resourced**
- **Different states need different movement**
- **Rest is medicine when depleted**
- **Forcing movement when exhausted causes harm**
- **Your body knows what it needs**
- **Context matters as much as movement type**
- **Progressive challenge only when ready**
- **Trust your body over any "should"**

When to Seek Support

Consider professional help if:

- You have panic disorder (need graduated exposure)
- Exercise has become compulsive
- You have chronic fatigue syndrome/ME
- You're exercising despite injury
- Movement consistently makes you worse
- You have an eating disorder
- You can't tell if movement helps or harms

Work with professionals who understand your condition.

Your Movement Bill of Rights

I have the right to:

• Need different movement on different days

• Rest when my body needs rest

• Discharge energy when activated

• Move gently when depleted

• Trust my body's signals

• Ignore "no pain, no gain" mentality

• Define movement broadly

• Seek help if needed

Signed: _____

Date: _____

End of Chapter 8 Workbook

Next: Part Three - Relationships as Practice

(From inner awareness to outer relationships)

END OF PART TWO

• • •

You've learned to work with patterns.

> **The Three-Step Pattern:**
>
> 1. Notice what's happening
>
> 2. Validate why it makes sense
>
> 3. Try tiny adjustment

You've practiced honoring capacity,
working with anxiety,
dialoguing with resistance,
choosing movement medicine.

Some experiments worked.
Some didn't.
Both taught you something.

• • •

*Part Three explores what happens
when other nervous systems enter the picture.*

Warning: Everything gets harder with others present.

That's not failure. That's the advanced practice.

PART THREE

Relationships as Practice

From inner awareness to outer relationships

Alone, I've mastered noticing.
Can catch anxiety rising, thank my night
guard, honor my capacity.

Then the phone rings.
Three words—not even critical—
just that familiar tone, and my shoulders
are at my ears.

That careful awareness? Gone.
The breathing practices? Forgotten.
I'm fourteen again, defending myself from
criticism that hasn't even come yet.

This is where the real practice begins—
not in the quiet of solitude
but in the storm of connection,
where other nervous systems crash into mine
and all my patterns wake at once.

Welcome to the Advanced Practice

You've built something real. Alone, you can notice patterns, validate them, make tiny adjustments. You've learned to work with your capacity, dialogue with your night guard, choose movement that matches your state.

Then your mother calls.

Or your partner walks in from work, and before they speak, your body is already matching their mood.

Or you're having a normal disagreement when suddenly you're your father—jaw set, walking away, silent treatment deployed.

This isn't failure. This is the difference between practicing scales alone and playing in an orchestra. The skills are the same, but now you're navigating multiple nervous systems at once.

• • •

The Truth About Relationships and Patterns

Your nervous system evolved to sync with others for survival. If one person in your ancient tribe sensed danger, everyone needed to activate quickly. "Oh, Bob's running? Maybe I should run too. Figure out why later."

This still happens. You're not just managing your patterns anymore. You're swimming in a sea of other people's patterns, all affecting yours without anyone choosing it.

This is why relationships are where the real practice happens:

- All your patterns activate simultaneously
- You catch emotions like colds
- Old wounds get triggered by present interactions
- Inherited patterns surface without warning
- Your carefully cultivated awareness evaporates

And this is normal. This is human. This is the work.

Your Journey Through Part Three

Chapter 9: The Space Between Us

You'll discover why you're either a doormat or dynamite with boundaries. Your body learned these tools before you could speak, and they activate faster than thought.

Practice focus: Noticing which boundary tool you reach for

Chapter 10: Bodies in the Same Room

Understanding how nervous systems sync without permission. You literally catch emotions from others, matching their states before you realize it's happening.

Practice focus: Conscious co-regulation

Chapter 11: The Relationship Mirror

When you understand syncing, you can recognize why strong reactions reveal old wounds. That rage about the dishwasher is actually information.

Practice focus: Using intensity as data

Chapter 12: Breaking Inherited Patterns

Those wounds often travel through generations. You hear your mother's words coming from your mouth. Three generations of "I love you, but..." stopping with you—if you can catch it.

Practice focus: Interrupting intergenerational patterns

Chapter 13: Living with Nervous System Awareness

Finally, learning to live with all this awareness without drowning in it. Finding the middle path between hypervigilance and unconscious repetition.

Practice focus: Integration without overwhelm

• • •

Why This Is Advanced Practice

Relationships activate everything at once:

The checking pattern you thought you'd mastered? Your mother's voice brings it back instantly.

The capacity awareness you developed? Gone the moment your partner gets stressed.

The breathing techniques that work alone? Impossible when someone's crying in front of you.

This is because:

- Mirror neurons fire without your permission

- Attachment patterns activate faster than thought

- Emotional contagion happens before awareness

- Power dynamics affect your nervous system

- Cultural conditioning runs deeper than individual work

Skills You'll Need from Parts One and Two

Check that you have at least some of these capacities:

- Can sometimes notice patterns while they're running

- Have found at least one neutral body spot

- Know the three-step pattern (notice-validate-adjust)

- Can recognize window versus keyhole days

- Sometimes catch yourself before automatic responses

- Have practiced validating before changing

If you have even 2-3 of these, you're ready for Part Three.

What Makes Part Three Different

You're not just noticing YOUR patterns anymore. You're noticing:

- How your patterns interact with others' patterns

- When you're syncing versus maintaining your center

- Which inherited patterns are rising

- How power dynamics affect your responses

- When cultural conditioning overrides individual awareness

Managing Expectations for Part Three

You won't perfect this. No one does.

But you'll start to notice the dance—sometimes even while you're dancing. And occasionally, just occasionally, you'll have enough awareness to choose a different step.

That moment of choice in relationship—when you catch yourself midpattern with another person present—that's where healing accelerates. Not because you handle it perfectly, but because you're finally working with patterns where they actually live: between nervous systems, not just within your own.

What "Success" Looks Like in Part Three

Success IS:
- *Noticing you're in a pattern WITH someone (even afterward)*
- *Catching yourself syncing with their anxiety (even if you can't stop)*
- *Recognizing inherited words as you say them*
- *Having 3 seconds of awareness during conflict*
- *Apologizing when patterns run anyway*

Success IS NOT:
- *Never getting triggered by family*
- *Perfect boundaries every time*
- *Never catching others' emotions*
- *Breaking all inherited patterns*
- *Constant awareness with others*

Part Three Reality Check:

Last week I had beautiful morning awareness. Noticed my capacity (medium), thanked my night guard, matched movement to my state. Felt regulated. Centered.

Then my assistant called about a crisis. Within thirty seconds I was activated, defensive, heard myself saying "I'll handle everything!" My shoulders screamed "delegate!" while my mouth promised to take on everyone's responsibilities.

All that morning awareness? Completely gone.

This is the advanced practice. Not preventing activation, but noticing it faster and recovering sooner.

● ● ●

Before You Begin Part Three

Take a breath. This part might feel overwhelming because relationships ARE overwhelming when you're aware of all the nervous system dynamics.

Remember:

- You don't need perfect awareness
- Noticing after the fact still counts
- Small moments of consciousness matter
- Repair is as important as prevention
- Everyone struggles with this part

Turn the page to begin Chapter 9: The Space Between Us Where you'll discover why you're either a doormat or dynamite, and how to find the tiny space where choice might live.

CHAPTER 9 WORKBOOK

The Space Between Us: Why You're Either a Doormat or Dynamite
(And How to Find the Middle)

SPEAKING IT TRUE - The Instant Response

Someone: *"Can you help me move this weekend?"*

Your mouth (before brain engages): *"Of course! Happy to!"*

Your shoulders: **Already at ears**

Your stomach: **Sinking**

Your actual availability: *Zero*

The truth: *"My body grabbed a tool before I could think"*

Welcome to Part Three: Relationships

You've learned to notice your patterns alone. Now comes the real challenge: maintaining awareness when other people are involved.

Chapter 9 focuses on boundaries - the three tools your body uses:

Doormat: Automatic yes to avoid conflict

Dynamite: Explosive no to create distance

Disappearing: Going blank when choice is needed

The goal isn't perfect boundaries - it's noticing which tool you're reaching for.

Quick Boundary Check

Someone just asked you for something. What happens in your body FIRST?

DOORMAT RESPONSE

- ☐ Immediate "yes" before thinking
- ☐ Shoulders rise to ears
- ☐ Stomach sinks
- ☐ Already planning how to do it
- ☐ Guilt if considering "no"

Learned: Saying no meant losing love/connection

DYNAMITE RESPONSE

- ☐ Heat floods chest
- ☐ Immediate anger
- ☐ Want to attack/push away
- ☐ "How dare they ask!"
- ☐ Ready to cut them off

Learned: Had to fight for everything

DISAPPEARING RESPONSE

- ☐ Mind goes blank
- ☐ Can't access yes or no
- ☐ Feel far away/floating
- ☐ Frozen, can't speak
- ☐ Need to escape

Learned: Neither yes nor no was safe

This Week's Boundary Tracking

Track which tool your body reaches for BEFORE you think:

Day	Who Asked	What They Wanted	Tool I Grabbed	When I Noticed
Monday				
Tuesday				
Wednesday				
Thursday				
Friday				
Saturday				
Sunday				

Tools: D = Doormat, Dy = Dynamite, Dis = Disappear | Notice: Before/During/After/Didn't

SPEAKING IT TRUE - The Space Between

The request: *Arrives*

The space: *0.5 seconds*

Your body: *Already grabbed a tool*

Your awareness: *"Wait, I see what's happening!"*

The practice: *"Let me think about that and get back to you"*

Finding the Space Between Trigger and Tool

Viktor Frankl wrote: "Between stimulus and response there is a space." That space is tiny but real.

The Space-Finding Practice

When someone makes a request:

1. **FEEL** your body's first response (shoulders? chest? stomach?)

2. **NOTICE** which tool it's reaching for

3. **NAME IT** internally: "There's my doormat/dynamite/disappear"

4. **BUY TIME**: "Let me think about that"

Practice phrases to buy time:

☐ "Let me check my schedule and get back to you"

☐ "I need to think about that"

☐ "Can I let you know tomorrow?"

☐ "That's interesting - let me consider it"

☐ "I need to check with [partner/calendar/energy]"

The phrase that feels most natural to me: _____

Understanding Your Doormat Pattern

If you're a doormat person, check what's true:

- ☐ I say yes before checking with my body
- ☐ I feel guilty for having needs
- ☐ Others' needs feel more important
- ☐ I resent commitments I made
- ☐ I often cancel last minute (overwhelmed)
- ☐ Disappointing others feels dangerous

The fear underneath: _____

Working with doormat pattern:

1. Notice shoulders rising = doormat activating

2. Say: "That's my doormat tool reaching for yes"

3. Buy time before responding

4. Check: "Do I actually want to do this?"

5. Practice: "That doesn't work for me" (even once)

Understanding Your Dynamite Pattern

If you're a dynamite person, check what's true:

☐ Requests feel like attacks

☐ I create maximum distance fast

☐ My no comes out harsh

☐ I cut people off completely

☐ Small boundaries become walls

☐ I'm often alone but protected

What the anger is protecting: _____

Working with dynamite pattern:

1. Notice heat rising = dynamite loading

2. Say: "That's my protective anger activating"

3. Ask: "What's the tender thing underneath?"

4. Buy time to cool down

5. Practice: Softer no from center, not armor

Understanding Your Disappearing Pattern

If you're a disappearer, check what's true:

☐ I literally can't find yes or no

☐ I leave my body when asked things

☐ I ghost rather than respond

☐ Decisions feel impossible

☐ I need lots of processing time

☐ Direct questions make me float away

Why neither yes nor no felt safe: _____

Working with disappearing pattern:

1. Notice floating = disappearing starting

2. Find neutral spot (Chapter 4) to anchor

3. Say: "I need time to find my answer"

4. Take the time you actually need

5. Practice: Give answer even if uncertain

SPEAKING IT TRUE - What's Under the Anger

Surface: *"HOW DARE THEY ASK ME THAT!"*

Under that: *"I'm scared they'll be mad if I say no"*

Under that: *"I'm sad that my needs don't matter"*

Under that: *"I'm exhausted from protecting myself"*

The truth: *"My anger guards tender places"*

Building New Tools (Gradually)

Between doormat and dynamite, there's a middle way:

TOOLS FROM CENTER (Not Armor)

The Information Tool:

"That doesn't work for me" (neutral information, not attack)

The Clarification Tool:

"Help me understand what you need" (buying time while staying engaged)

The Partial Tool:

"I can do X but not Y" (meeting partway)

The Timeline Tool:

"I can't this week but could next month" (if true)

The Honesty Tool:

"I want to say yes but my capacity is zero" (vulnerable truth)

Proactive vs Reactive Boundaries

Reactive Boundaries (This Chapter)

Happen in the moment when someone asks something

Body responds before mind

Tangled with fear/guilt/anger

Example: "Can you help me move?" → Automatic yes while shoulders tense

Proactive Boundaries (Easier!)

Decided in advance when calm

Based on values/needs

Communicated from center

Example: "I don't take work calls after 7 PM" (already decided)

Proactive boundaries I already have:

1. _____

2. _____

Proactive boundaries I want to create:

1. _____

2. _____

Your Boundary Experiments This Week

Pick ONE to practice:

- [ ] Notice my body's response before answering
- [ ] Say "Let me think about that" once
- [ ] Practice one "That doesn't work for me"
- [ ] Notice which tool I reach for most
- [ ] Ask "What is my anger protecting?"
- [ ] Set one proactive boundary

The experiment I choose: _____

With whom I'll practice: _____

Weekly Reflection

After tracking boundaries this week:

My most common tool: _____

I notice it activates most with: _____

The earliest I caught it: _____

What surprised me:

What I'm protecting myself from:

One tiny success:

Important Reminders

- **These tools kept you safe once** - they're not character flaws

- **Your body responds faster than thought** - that's normal

- **The space between trigger and tool exists** - even if tiny

- **Noticing after the fact still counts** as progress

- **Some days you'll use old tools** - that's okay

- **Anger often protects vulnerability**

- **Practice with safe people first**

- **Progress is noticing, not perfection**

When Boundaries Need Professional Support

Seek help if:

- You're in an abusive relationship

- Boundaries trigger severe panic/dissociation

- You can never say no (or only say no)

- Boundary issues significantly impact relationships

- You're unsafe when setting boundaries

Safety comes first. Get support if needed.

End of Chapter 9 Workbook

Next: Chapter 10 - Bodies in the Same Room

(How nervous systems sync without permission)

CHAPTER 10 WORKBOOK

Bodies in the Same Room: How Nervous Systems Sync Without Permission

SPEAKING IT TRUE - Emotional Contagion

Your partner: *Walks in stressed*

Your body (before they speak): *Shoulders rising to match*

Five minutes later: *Both irritated, neither knows why*

The truth: *"We're syncing without choosing to"*

Welcome to Emotional Contagion

You've learned to notice your boundary patterns. Now Chapter 10 explores what happens when nervous systems meet - how you catch emotions like colds.

The key discovery: Bodies affect each other automatically through:

Mirror neurons that fire when observing others

Quick Contagion Check

Think of the last time you were with someone stressed. Check what happened:

Their State → Your Response

- [ ] My breathing changed to match theirs
- [ ] My shoulders rose when theirs were tense
- [ ] I felt their anxiety in my chest
- [ ] Their mood became my mood
- [ ] I was fine before they arrived
- [ ] I was exhausted after they left
- [ ] I didn't notice any change (also valid!)

The person whose emotions I catch most: _____

The emotion I'm most likely to catch: _____

Important: Not everyone experiences emotional contagion the same way. If you have autism, ADHD, or are highly sensitive, your experience might be completely different. There's no "right" way to sync or not sync.

This Week's Syncing Tracker

Track when you catch someone's emotional state:

Day	Who I Was With	Their State	What I Caught	When I Noticed
Monday				
Tuesday				
Wednesday				
Thursday				
Friday				
Saturday				
Sunday				

Notice: Before/During/After/Didn't notice

SPEAKING IT TRUE - The Choice Point

Before they arrive: *"I'm calm, centered"*

They walk in activated: *"I feel my body starting to match..."*

The choice point: *"Do I sync or stay centered?"*

The practice: *"I can offer my calm without joining their storm"*

The Before/During/After Practice

Conscious Co-Regulation Exercise

BEFORE someone arrives:

- [ ] Quick body check - where am I starting?
- [ ] Notice: shoulders, breathing, general mood
- [ ] Mental note: "This is my baseline"

WHEN they arrive:

- [ ] Notice their state without judging
- [ ] Feel if your body starts matching
- [ ] Ask internally: "Do I want to sync?"

IF you choose to stay centered:

- [ ] Three deep breaths
- [ ] Feel feet on floor
- [ ] Maintain your rhythm
- [ ] Offer your calm as a resource

AFTER they leave:

- [ ] Check: Did I maintain center?
- [ ] If not, shake it off (literally)
- [ ] Reset to your baseline

Understanding Your Sensitivity Level

Are You an Emotional Sponge?

High Sensitivity (15-20% of people):

- [ ] I absorb everyone's emotions
- [ ] Crowds exhaust me
- [ ] I need alone time to reset
- [ ] I feel others' pain physically
- [ ] I know someone's mood before they speak

Moderate Sensitivity:

- [ ] I catch strong emotions
- [ ] Some people affect me more
- [ ] I can usually maintain boundaries
- [ ] Recovery time varies

Lower Sensitivity:

- [ ] Others' moods don't affect me much
- [ ] I maintain my state easily
- [ ] I might not notice others' emotions
- [ ] This isn't better or worse - just different

My sensitivity level seems to be:

This means I need: _____

When Syncing Serves

Sometimes matching someone's state is exactly right:

Healthy Syncing Moments

When to sync:

- Friend grieving - matching their sadness shows "you're not alone"

- Child excited - matching their joy amplifies connection

- Partner needs validation - matching their frustration shows solidarity

- Celebration time - shared joy builds bonds

When to stay separate:

- Someone's panic that isn't based in reality

- Chronic negativity that depletes you

- Disproportionate anger

- Others' anxiety about things outside control

The key question: Will syncing serve connection or create two dysregulated people?

People Who Affect Your State

Instead of labeling people as "toxic" or "energy vampires," let's be more specific:

People/situations that often leave me depleted:

People who help me feel grounded:

Note: Someone who depletes you might be in crisis and need professional support, not avoidance. This isn't about them being "bad."

Protection Without Walls

Strategies for Different Sensitivity Levels

For Moderate Sensitivity:

- Notice when you're syncing
- Take bathroom breaks to reset
- Use grounding (feet on floor)
- Name it: "I'm matching your anxiety"

For High Sensitivity:

- Limit time with dysregulated people
- Schedule recovery after interactions
- Consider if certain relationships are sustainable
- Work with therapist on energetic boundaries
- Remember: needing more boundaries isn't weakness

For Lower Sensitivity:

- Your stability can be a gift to others
- Watch for not noticing when others need support
- Practice tuning in occasionally
- Don't judge those who sync more easily

Remember: Your calm is contagious too. When you're genuinely regulated, others can "borrow" your state. But it's not your job to regulate everyone around you.

Your Co-Regulation Experiments

Pick ONE to practice this week:

- [ ] Do before/after check-ins with one person
- [ ] Practice staying centered when someone's activated
- [ ] Notice who you sync with most
- [ ] Try one bathroom reset
- [ ] Offer your calm without forcing it
- [ ] Shake off someone's energy after they leave

The experiment I choose: _____

I'll practice with: _____

Weekly Reflection

After tracking emotional contagion:

I catch emotions most from: _____

The emotion I catch most easily: _____

I maintained my center when:

One thing that helped me stay centered:

What surprised me about emotional contagion:

Cultural & Individual Considerations

Remember these variations:

Cultural differences:

- Some cultures value emotional synchrony as harmony

- Others prize maintaining individual emotional states

- Neither is right or wrong

Neurodivergent differences:

- Autism may mean less automatic syncing

- ADHD might mean difficulty filtering others' emotions

- HSP (Highly Sensitive Person) means deeper processing

In relationships:

- Some syncing is healthy and necessary

- Complete non-syncing feels disconnected

- Complete syncing is exhausting

- Find your balance

Important Reminders

- Nervous systems sync automatically - it's not a choice initially

- Noticing you're syncing is the first step to choosing

- Sometimes syncing serves connection

- Sometimes staying centered serves better

- You can offer your calm as a resource (when you have it)

- Some people will affect you more - that's information

- Protection doesn't require walls, just awareness

- You'll still get pulled in sometimes - that's human

End of Chapter 10 Workbook

Next: Chapter 11 - The Relationship Mirror

(What strong reactions reveal about old wounds)

CHAPTER 11 WORKBOOK

The Relationship Mirror: What Strong Reactions Reveal

SPEAKING IT TRUE - The 10/90 Rule

The trigger: *Partner leaves dish in sink*

Your reaction: *VOLCANIC RAGE*

The math: *10% about the dish, 90% about something else*

The truth: *"This intensity is information"*

Understanding Intensity

Chapter 11 explores what happens when your reaction is way bigger than the moment warrants. That rage about the spoon? That panic from a compliment? Your body might be showing you where old wounds live.

Important: This is ONE framework for understanding reactions, not the only explanation. Sometimes intense reactions are completely appropriate to current situations.

Quick Intensity Check

Which of these trigger outsized reactions in you?

- ☐ Being interrupted
- ☐ Running late / others being late
- ☐ Receiving criticism
- ☐ Being told what to do
- ☐ Mess/disorder
- ☐ Being ignored or overlooked
- ☐ Authority figures
- ☐ Money discussions
- ☐ Any conflict
- ☐ Receiving praise
- ☐ Making mistakes
- ☐ Asking for help
- ☐ Being misunderstood
- ☐ Changes in plans

Pattern I notice: _____

These might be touching: _____

Remember: Having intense reactions doesn't mean something's wrong with you. People with ADHD often experience emotional dysregulation. Highly sensitive people feel everything more deeply. Some cultures express emotions more intensely. Your intensity might be your normal.

Mapping a Recent Intense Reaction

Think of a time recently when you had a HUGE reaction to something relatively small:

The Reaction Analysis

What happened (the facts):

My reaction (what I did/said/felt):

Intensity level:

1	2	3	4	5	6	7	8	9	10

Circle your intensity level

Where I felt it in my body:

☐ Chest (tight, heavy, burning)

☐ Throat (closed, choked)

☐ Stomach (knots, nausea)

☐ Head (pressure, pain)

☐ Whole body (vibrating, hot)

☐ Other: _____

This feeling is familiar from: _____

SPEAKING IT TRUE - Multiple Factors

Surface: *"They were 5 minutes late!"*

Current factor: *"This is the third time this week"*

Past factor: *"Being forgotten/not mattering"*

Physical factor: *"I haven't eaten in 6 hours"*

The truth: *"It's usually ALL of these at once"*

The Multiple Factors Assessment

Intense reactions usually have multiple causes. For your recent reaction, check ALL that contributed:

Current Factors

- [ ] I was already stressed
- [ ] I was exhausted
- [ ] I was hungry ("hangry")
- [ ] This was the 5th time it happened
- [ ] Hormonal factors
- [ ] I was already overwhelmed
- [ ] Work/life stress was high
- [ ] Multiple things went wrong that day
- [ ] Other: _____

Possible Past Connections

- [ ] This reminds me of childhood experiences
- [ ] I've felt this exact feeling before when...
- [ ] This touches an old worry about being...
- [ ] Someone used to do this same thing
- [ ] This pattern runs in my family

Systemic/Ongoing Issues

- [ ] This is part of an ongoing pattern
- [ ] There's a real issue here that needs addressing
- [ ] Power dynamics are involved
- [ ] My boundaries are being crossed repeatedly

The 10/90 Framework (One Tool, Not THE Truth)

This is the author's personal framework for thinking about reactions, not a scientific rule:

Your Reaction Math

For the reaction you mapped:

_____ % about the present moment

_____ % about other factors (past, physical, accumulated stress)

= **100%** of your reaction

BUT REMEMBER:

- Sometimes it's 100% present and 0% past
- Sometimes you're legitimately angry about the actual thing
- Sometimes the "small" thing is part of a big pattern
- This framework is ONE way to think about it, not THE way

Don't Use This Framework To:

- Dismiss your legitimate concerns
- Avoid addressing real problems
- Let someone gaslight you about your reactions
- Invalidate your feelings
- Overanalyze every emotion

Sometimes the dishes really ARE the problem!

This Week's Intensity Tracker

Track your strong reactions without judgment:

Day	Trigger	Intensity (1-10)	Current vs Other Factors	What I Learned
Monday				
Tuesday				
Wednesday				
Thursday				
Friday				

Current vs Other: Note if reaction was mostly about now or included other factors

Working With Intensity

The Three-Step Response to Strong Reactions

1. VALIDATE the intensity:

- "This feeling is real and powerful"
- "My body is having a strong response"
- Don't immediately call it "overreacting"

2. GET CURIOUS about sources:

- "Is this about something current that needs addressing?"
- "Is exhaustion/stress/hunger amplifying this?"
- "Does this connect to past experiences?"
- "Is this my baseline (HSP, ADHD)?"
- "Are multiple factors combining?"

3. RESPOND to what you find:

- Current problem → Address it directly
- Physical needs → Eat, rest, restore
- Past connection → Notice with compassion
- Mixed causes → Acknowledge all factors

The Both/And Reality: Your reaction probably has multiple causes. Past AND present. Physical state AND emotional trigger. Individual temperament AND situational factors. All can be true at once.

When Intensity Is Completely Appropriate

Before you search for "old wounds," check if your reaction is actually spot-on:

Is This Reaction Actually Appropriate?

- ☐ Someone repeatedly violates stated boundaries
- ☐ You're responding to actual disrespect
- ☐ This is part of an ongoing pattern you've addressed
- ☐ You're dealing with real unfairness/discrimination
- ☐ Multiple "small" things have accumulated
- ☐ Your body is accurately warning about real threat
- ☐ The situation genuinely warrants strong response

If you checked any of these: Your intensity might be completely justified. Don't use this framework to dismiss legitimate reactions.

Important for women especially: You're often told you're "overreacting" when responding appropriately to real issues. Trust yourself.

Cultural & Individual Differences

Remember:

- Some cultures express emotions more intensely - that's normal expression, not overreacting

- ADHD often includes rejection sensitive dysphoria - intense responses to perceived rejection

- HSPs feel everything more deeply - it's neurological, not drama

- Neurodivergent people may have different emotional regulation

- Your normal might be someone else's "too much" - that's okay

Your Intensity Experiments This Week

Choose ONE to practice:

☐ Track intensity levels without trying to change them

☐ Ask "What factors are contributing?" for one reaction

☐ Validate intensity before analyzing it

☐ Notice patterns in what triggers big reactions

☐ Try the 24-hour wait before responding to intensity

☐ Share one reaction pattern with trusted friend

The experiment I choose: _____

Weekly Reflection

After tracking intensity this week:

My most common intensity triggers:

My most common intensity triggers:

☐ Current stressors

☐ Past patterns

☐ Physical factors (tired/hungry)

☐ All of the above

One reaction that was completely appropriate:

One reaction that had multiple factors:

What this teaches me about my patterns:

When to Seek Support

Consider Professional Help If:

- Every small thing triggers huge reactions

- You can't recover from emotional intensity

- Your reactions damage relationships

- You feel constantly triggered

- You can't tell if reactions are proportionate

- Intensity includes self-harm thoughts

- You're exhausted from emotional storms

This isn't weakness - it's recognizing when patterns need more support than self-help provides.

Important Final Reminders

- Strong reactions usually have multiple causes

- The 10/90 framework is one lens, not the only truth

- Sometimes intensity is completely appropriate

- Current stress matters as much as old patterns

- Different people have different emotional baselines

- Curiosity beats shame every time

- Don't let self-analysis avoid addressing real problems

- Trust yourself when something feels genuinely wrong

End of Chapter 11 Workbook

Next: Chapter 12 - Breaking Inherited Patterns

(How generational patterns show up in your relationships)

CHAPTER 12 WORKBOOK

Breaking Inherited Patterns: How Generational Trauma Shows Up in Your Relationships

SPEAKING IT TRUE - Three Generations, One Sentence

Your grandmother: *"I love you, but you could do better"*

Your mother: *"I love you, but you could do better"*

You (catching yourself): *"I love y— wait, that's not my voice"*

The truth: *"I can choose which patterns die with me"*

Understanding Inherited Patterns

Chapter 12 explores how relationship patterns travel through generations. You don't just inherit eye color - you inherit ways of loving, fighting, and being in the world.

Important: Patterns are transmitted through multiple pathways - genetics, learned behavior, environmental factors, and often all three. Correlation doesn't equal causation. Similar patterns might have different sources.

Family Pattern Inventory

Check the patterns you recognize in your family line (these could be genetic, learned, or both):

Relationship Patterns

- [ ] Conflict avoidance (peace at any price)
- [ ] Explosive reactions (0 to 100)
- [ ] Emotional withdrawal (leaving when feelings arise)
- [ ] Hypervigilance (constant scanning for danger)
- [ ] Conditional love ("I love you, but...")
- [ ] Perfectionism (never good enough)
- [ ] Enmeshment (no boundaries)

- [ ] Emotional absence (work over presence)
- [ ] Silent treatment (withdrawal as weapon)
- [ ] Guilt as control ("If you loved me...")
- [ ] Anxiety/worry patterns
- [ ] Depression/low mood tendencies
- [ ] Caretaking at own expense
- [ ] Inability to express affection

Inherited Strengths (Don't Forget These!)

- [ ] Humor in hard times
- [ ] Persistence through challenges
- [ ] Creative problem-solving
- [ ] Ways of showing love
- [ ] Resilience strategies
- [ ] Cultural wisdom

- [ ] Survival skills
- [ ] Connection rituals
- [ ] Storytelling abilities
- [ ] Other:

_____

Your Generational Map

GRANDPARENTS' GENERATION

Patterns I've heard about or observed:

_____

_____

↓

PARENTS' GENERATION

What they inherited/developed:

_____

_____

↓

YOUR GENERATION

What you inherited/changed:

_____

_____

↓

NEXT GENERATION

What you're passing on/changing:

_____

_____

Remember: You might share patterns due to genetics, learning, similar environments, or coincidence. Don't assume direct transmission. Also, siblings often develop completely different patterns despite the same parents.

SPEAKING IT TRUE - The Interrupt

The moment: *You hear your parent's words coming out*

The catch: *"Wait, I'm doing that thing..."*

The interrupt: *"Sorry, that was my mom's voice. Let me try again"*

The choice: *Pattern acknowledged, different response chosen*

Identifying Your Inherited Patterns

Pattern Recognition Exercise

Think of ONE specific pattern you inherited:

The pattern: _____

I notice it when:

Words that rise automatically:

Body sensations that accompany it:

- [ ] Shoulders rising
- [ ] Jaw clenching
- [ ] Stomach tightening
- [ ] Voice changing tone
- [ ] Energy shifting
- [ ] Other: _____

Who I sound/act like: _____

How this pattern might have been adaptive for them:

Understanding Multiple Sources

For the pattern you identified, consider ALL possible sources:

Where Did This Pattern Come From?

Genetic factors (tendencies you might have inherited):

- ☐ Anxiety sensitivity
- ☐ Emotional regulation style
- ☐ Stress response patterns
- ☐ Temperament traits
- ☐ Processing differences

Learned through observation:

- ☐ Watched parent(s) do this repeatedly
- ☐ This was modeled as "normal"
- ☐ Absorbed without words
- ☐ Copied to gain approval

Response to similar stressors:

- ☐ We faced similar challenges
- ☐ Same environmental pressures
- ☐ Cultural/societal factors
- ☐ Economic similarities

My unique interpretation:

- ☐ I adapted it differently
- ☐ Combined with my temperament
- ☐ Influenced by peers/partners
- ☐ Modified by my experiences

Key Point: You're not a passive recipient. You're actively choosing consciously or unconsciously - which patterns to keep, modify, or reject. You have agency.

The Pattern Interrupt Practice

Catching and Changing Inherited Patterns

Choose ONE inherited pattern to work with this week:

The pattern I'll watch for: _____

How I'll recognize it starting:

Body signal: _____

Familiar words: _____

Energy shift: _____

My interrupt phrases (choose one that feels natural):

☐ "Wait, that's my mother's/father's voice"

☐ "I'm doing that thing again"

☐ "This is the old pattern"

☐ "Let me choose differently"

☐ "That's not actually what I want to say"

☐ Other: _____

What I'll choose instead:

Remember: You won't catch it every time. Progress is noticing it sometimes, not perfection.

This Week's Pattern Tracking

Noticing after the fact is still progress. Your brain is building new pathways each time you recognize a pattern.

Day	Pattern I Noticed	Whose Voice/ Behavior	Caught It?	What Happened
Monday			Before/During/ After	
Tuesday			Before/During/ After	
Wednesday			Before/During/ After	
Thursday			Before/During/ After	
Friday			Before/During/ After	

The Both/And Practice

For each inherited pattern, practice holding complexity:

Holding Multiple Truths

Pattern: _____

I inherited this tendency AND I have choice about it.

Pattern: _____

This came from my family AND I'm reshaping it.

Pattern: _____

I understand why they had this AND I can choose differently.

Pattern: _____

This might be partly genetic AND I can still work with it.

Compassion Without Excusing

Understanding Your Parents' Patterns

My mother/primary caregiver gave me certain patterns because:

- [ ] That's what she knew
- [ ] She was doing her best with what she had
- [ ] She inherited them too
- [ ] She was surviving her own challenges
- [ ] That's what worked in her experience
- [ ] She didn't have the tools to do differently

My father/other caregiver gave me certain patterns because:

- [ ] That's what he knew
- [ ] He was doing his best with what he had
- [ ] He inherited them too
- [ ] He was surviving his own challenges
- [ ] That's what worked in his experience
- [ ] He didn't have the tools to do differently

I can have compassion for them while still:

- [ ] Choosing differently
- [ ] Protecting myself if needed
- [ ] Healing what hurts
- [ ] Breaking cycles
- [ ] Setting boundaries

What You're Changing for the Next Generation

Your Legacy Work

If you have or might have children:

Patterns I want to pass on:

Patterns I'm actively changing:

New patterns I'm creating:

If you don't have children:

Patterns I'm changing in all my relationships:

How I'm influencing others (friends, nieces/nephews, community):

You're already changing patterns for future generations, whether or not you have children.

Weekly Reflection

After working with inherited patterns this week:

The pattern I noticed most:

A moment I caught myself mid-pattern:

A time I chose differently:

An inherited strength I used:

What I'm learning about agency and choice:

When to Seek Support

Consider therapy for inherited patterns when:

- You keep recreating dynamics you hate

- You can't interrupt patterns even when you notice them

- Inherited trauma significantly impacts relationships

- You're afraid to have children because of what you might pass on

- You need help building "earned secure attachment"

- Family patterns include addiction or abuse

Therapists can help sort out what's genetic, what's learned, what's current, and what you want to change.

Important Final Reminders

- Patterns transmit through genetics, behavior, and environment - usually all three

- Correlation doesn't equal causation

- 75% attachment correspondence means 25% develop different patterns

- Siblings often have completely different patterns

- You inherit strengths and resilience, not just wounds

- You actively interpret patterns, not passively receive them

- Neuroplasticity means change is possible throughout life

- "Earned secure attachment" is achievable

- You have agency in choosing which patterns continue

- Some patterns you'll interrupt easily, others take years

- Some inherited patterns are worth keeping

Your Agency Checkpoint

Remember your power:

- ☐ I inherited tendencies, not destinies
- ☐ My brain can form new patterns throughout life
- ☐ I actively interpret what I inherited
- ☐ I'm influenced by more than just my parents
- ☐ I have genetic traits AND behavioral choices
- ☐ Some patterns serve me and I can keep them
- ☐ Some patterns don't and I can change them
- ☐ Every moment of awareness creates possibility

End of Chapter 12 Workbook

Next: Chapter 13 - Living with Nervous System Awareness

(Integration without overwhelm - finding the middle path)

CHAPTER 13 WORKBOOK

Living with Nervous System Awareness: Integration Without Overwhelm

SPEAKING IT TRUE - The Middle Path

Too much awareness: *"I'm tracking every breath, monitoring each heartbeat"*

Too little awareness: *"Patterns running wild, body screaming unheard"*

The middle path: *"Noticing when it matters, forgetting when it doesn't"*

The truth: *"Integration means living while aware, not living to be aware"*

Welcome to Integration

You've built awareness. You've practiced noticing patterns, working with capacity, understanding boundaries, recognizing inheritance. Now comes the real question: How do you live with this awareness without becoming obsessed with it?

The truth: Awareness can become its own prison. You can get so good at tracking your nervous system that you forget to live.

Your Current Awareness Level

Where are you on the awareness spectrum right now?

Too Much (Hypervigilance)	Just Right (Integration)	Too Little (Unconscious)
• Analyzing every sensation	• Notice when it matters	• Patterns run completely
• Can't enjoy things	• Can forget for hours	• Only notice after crashes
• Exhausted from tracking	• Brief check-ins enough	• Body signals surprise me
• Awareness creates anxiety	• Awareness helps navigate	• Same problems repeat

Check where you are TODAY:

☐ Hypervigilant - tracking everything

☐ Leaning toward too much awareness

☐ Pretty balanced

☐ Could use more awareness

☐ Mostly unconscious

☐ It varies day to day (most common!)

Note: Most of us swing between all three. That's normal and expected. The goal is to spend more time in the middle, not to stay there perfectly.

Signs You've Tipped Into Hypervigilance

Too Much Awareness Checklist

You might be overdoing awareness if:

- [ ] You analyze everyone's nervous system state constantly
- [ ] You're exhausted from tracking patterns all day
- [ ] Your awareness practice creates more anxiety
- [ ] You've stopped enjoying things (too busy noticing)
- [ ] Every sensation becomes a problem to solve
- [ ] You judge yourself for not being aware enough
- [ ] You judge yourself for being too aware
- [ ] You can't remember last time you just... existed
- [ ] Conversations become nervous system analysis sessions
- [ ] You've lost spontaneity

If you checked more than 3: Time to ease up. Way up. Awareness should serve life, not dominate it.

Signs You're in the Sweet Spot

Healthy Integration Checklist

☐ Patterns noticed when they matter, missed when they don't

☐ Awareness available but not always active

☐ Can forget about nervous system for hours

☐ Enjoying experiences while occasionally noticing

☐ Using awareness to navigate challenges, not create them

☐ Sometimes completely unconscious (and that's fine)

☐ Brief check-ins feel sufficient

☐ Can be spontaneous again

SPEAKING IT TRUE - The 5-3-1 Rule

Morning: *5-second body scan*

During day: *3 transition check-ins*

Evening: *1-minute reflection*

Total time: *Less than 5 minutes*

The truth: *"That's enough. Really."*

Your Personal 5-3-1 Practice

Design Your Minimal Effective Dose

My 5-second morning check happens:

☐ While coffee brews

☐ Before getting out of bed

☐ In the shower

☐ During commute

☐ Other: _____

My 3 transition moments are:

1. _____

2. _____

3. _____

(Examples: bathroom breaks, before meals, getting in car, between meetings)

My 1-minute evening reflection happens:

☐ While brushing teeth

☐ In bed before sleep

☐ After dinner

☐ During evening walk

☐ Other:

Total daily awareness practice: Under 5 minutes

Declaring Your Awareness-Free Zones

Choose 3-5 activities where you deliberately practice NO awareness:

My Awareness-Free Zones

☐ Watching movies/TV

☐ Playing with kids/pets

☐ Exercise/sports

☐ Sex/intimacy

☐ Creative activities (art, music, writing)

☐ Gaming

☐ Reading for pleasure

☐ Cooking

☐ Time in nature

☐ Conversations with _____

☐ Other: _____

☐ Other: _____

Permission granted to be completely unconscious during these activities.

The Weekly Rhythm

A Sustainable Practice Schedule

Monday-Friday: Normal life with brief check-ins (5-3-1)

Saturday: One longer practice session if desired (10-20 min)

Sunday: Complete awareness break - live unconsciously on purpose

My weekly rhythm will be:

This prevents both extremes: neglecting awareness AND obsessing over it.

Integration Troubleshooting

Common Challenges & Solutions

Which is your biggest challenge?

☐ **I forget everything under stress**
→ That's normal. Success is remembering faster afterward, not perfect awareness during.

☐ **I can't stop monitoring everything**
→ Set a timer. 5 minutes awareness, then mandatory break. Build unconscious time.

☐ **My partner/friends think this is weird**
→ Use normal language. "I'm stressed" not "I'm dysregulated." Results matter more than terminology.

☐ **Nothing seems to change despite awareness**
→ Awareness isn't magic. It informs other changes - therapy, medication, lifestyle. What else might help?

☐ **I judge myself constantly**
→ The judgment is just another pattern. "Oh, hello inner critic about my awareness. You're a pattern too."

☐ **I swing between hypervigilance and oblivion**
→ Normal! The swinging will gradually decrease. Middle ground develops slowly.

When Awareness Disappears (And That's Okay)

You'll lose all awareness during:

- Crises (survival mode takes over)

- Intense joy (presence takes over)

- Deep focus (flow state takes over)

- Exhaustion (nothing left to notice with)

- Conflict (patterns run automatically)

This is NORMAL. Integration isn't maintaining perfect awareness. It's noticing when you can, forgetting when you can't, and not judging either.

Finding Your People

Building Community Support

Who in your life might understand this work?

People who might understand "window/keyhole days":

Someone I could share patterns with:

Online communities to explore:

Professional support I'm considering:

Even one person who gets it changes everything.

The Reality Check

Honest Assessment

Answer honestly:

Has awareness work become another way to feel broken?

☐ Yes ☐ No ☐ Sometimes

Do I spend more time monitoring than living?

☐ Yes ☐ No ☐ Sometimes

Am I kinder to myself since starting this work?

☐ Yes ☐ No ☐ Sometimes

Can I forget about patterns and just enjoy things?

☐ Yes ☐ No ☐ Sometimes

If you answered "No" to the last two: Time to ease up. Awareness should increase compassion and presence, not decrease them.

Your Integration Timeline

The Long-Term Journey

Integration happens in spirals, not straight lines:

Year 1: Excited about awareness, practice constantly, overwhelm yourself, back off

Year 2: Find rhythm, forget for months, remember again, gentler practice

Year 3: Natural rhythm emerges, awareness becomes background hum

Year 4+: Use awareness when needed, forget when not, no longer "practicing" - just living with more choice

Where I am now: _____

What I'm learning about my rhythm:

What Success Actually Looks Like

Integrated awareness ISN'T:

Constant monitoring • Never having patterns • Perfect regulation • Always conscious

• • •

Integrated awareness IS:

Noticing enough to have choice sometimes • Patterns running with less intensity • Recovering faster when activated • Remembering you have tools (even if you forget to use them) • Being kind to yourself about the whole messy process

PERMISSION SLIP

I give myself permission to:

☐ Forget everything I've learned

☐ Have patterns forever

☐ Stop monitoring

☐ Be unconscious sometimes

☐ Be imperfect at awareness

☐ Find this work weird

☐ Take breaks from noticing

☐ Sometimes use old patterns

☐ Not fix everything

☐ Be human

Signed: _____

Date: _____

This permission is valid forever and can be renewed as needed.

Your Integration Practice This Week

Pick just ONE to try:

☐ The 5-3-1 practice (5 sec morning, 3 quick checks, 1 min evening)

☐ One awareness-free activity daily

☐ Share one pattern with someone ("I noticed I do this thing...")

☐ Notice without fixing (just observe, no pressure to change)

☐ Catch yourself monitoring and gently stop

☐ Forget about all of this for a day and see what happens

☐ Practice being kind when awareness fails

The ONE thing I'll try: _____

Weekly Reflection

At week's end, notice:

Days I was hypervigilant: _____

Days I found balance: _____

Days I was mostly unconscious: _____

What helped me find balance:

When awareness served me:

When I successfully forgot to be aware:

Your Long-Term Vision

Integration Goals

In one year, I hope my awareness practice looks like:

Signs I'll know I've found balance:

What I want to remember when I forget everything:

Final Reminders

- The middle path between hypervigilance and oblivion is narrow andpersonal
- Brief check-ins work better than constant monitoring
- 5-3-1 rule: Total of less than 5 minutes daily is enough
- Awareness-free zones are essential for integration
- Losing awareness during stress is normal, not failure
- Community makes integration easier
- Success is having choice sometimes, not awareness always
- Integration happens in spirals over years
- Be gentle with yourself about the whole process

The goal was never to become a nervous system monitoring machine. It was to have enough awareness to make conscious choices when it matters, and to forget about it entirely when it doesn't.

Some days you'll track everything.
Some days you'll track nothing.
Most days you'll land somewhere in between.

That's the middle path.
That's integration.
That's enough.

End of Chapter 13 Workbook

End of Part Three

End of Workbook

You've completed the journey from awareness to integration.
The real practice begins now - living with just enough consciousness
to have choice when it matters.

Remember: You don't need perfect awareness.
You just need enough to occasionally notice what's happening.
That occasional noticing is the doorway to everything.

Keep noticing. Keep forgetting. Keep being human.
The work continues as long as we're breathing.

This Workbook Is NOT Appropriate If You're Experiencing:

- **Active thoughts of self-harm or suicide**

- **Plans to hurt yourself or others**

- **Severe dissociation or feeling disconnected from reality**

- **Psychosis or hallucinations**

- **Severe panic that won't subside**

- **Inability to care for yourself (eating, sleeping, hygiene)**

- **Substance use that feels out of control**

If any of these apply, please seek immediate professional help.

When to Work with a Professional Alongside This Workbook:

- Your patterns significantly interfere with daily life

- You have diagnosed mental health conditions

- You're processing significant trauma

- Exercises consistently increase your distress

- You feel overwhelmed by the material

- You want additional support while doing this work

This workbook can complement therapy but should never replace it.

Important to Remember:

Seeking help is not failure—it's wisdom.

Some patterns are too deep, too protective, or too necessary to shift withself-help alone. If you're struggling, that doesn't mean you're doing theexercises wrong. It might mean you need more support than a book canprovide.

Use this workbook while also working with:

- Therapists or counselors

- Support groups

- Psychiatrists for medication support

- Trauma specialists

- Other mental health professionals

• • •

Additional Resources

To find a therapist:
- Psychology Today Therapist Directory
- Your insurance provider's mental health network
- Local community mental health centers
- Employee Assistance Programs (EAP) through work

For specific types of support:
- SAMHSA National Helpline: 1-800-662-4357
- RAINN Sexual Assault Hotline: 1-800-656-4673
- National Domestic Violence Hotline: 1-800-799-7233
- Veterans Crisis Line: 1-800-273-8255, Press 1

International crisis lines:
- findahelpline.com (directory by country)
- iasp.info/resources/Crisis_Centres

Your life has value. You matter. Help is available.

If you're reading this page because you're struggling, please reach out for support. You don't have to do this alone.

PRIVACY AND PERSONAL USE

Your Work in This Book Belongs to You

YOUR PRIVACY IS ABSOLUTE

Everything you write in this workbook is completely private.

- Your responses, reflections, and discoveries belong only to you

- You are never obligated to share your workbook with anyone

- No one—not therapists, family, friends, or partners—has a right to readyour work

- You choose what to share, when to share it, and with whom

- Your healing journey is yours alone

This is your safe space to be completely honest without fear of judgment.

Personal Use Guidelines

This Workbook Is for YOUR Personal Use

We want you to use this workbook in whatever way serves your healing:

- **Write directly in it** - It's meant to be used, not kept pristine

- **Return to exercises** as many times as you need

- **Skip sections** that don't resonate

- **Work at your own pace** - There's no timeline

- **Start over** if you want a fresh beginning

Remember: No one will ever see what you write unless youchoose to show them. This workbook is your private companion on your journey.

• • •

Reproduction and Sharing Guidelines

WHAT YOU CAN DO

- **Make photocopies of individual pages** for your personal use only

- **Copy specific exercises** to carry with you (like emergency practices)

- **Create backup copies** of pages you use frequently

- **Share your experience** with the workbook (without reproducing content)

- **Recommend the workbook** to others who might benefit

- **Quote brief excerpts** in personal journals or therapy (with attribution)

- **Take photos of YOUR completed exercises** for your own reference

Personal photocopying is allowed because we understand you might want to:

- Redo exercises as you grow

- Keep certain practices accessible

- Have a clean copy if you want to start fresh

WHAT REQUIRES PERMISSION

- **Reproducing the entire workbook** or substantial portions

- **Sharing digital copies** or scans with others

- **Posting workbook content** on social media or websites

- **Using exercises** in group settings without permission

- **Incorporating content** into other materials or curricula

- **Making copies for others** (they need their own workbook)

- **Using commercially** in any way

For permissions, contact: phlabs.org

Why These Restrictions Matter

- These guidelines exist to:

- Protect the integrity of the healing process

- Ensure everyone has their own private workbook

- Maintain the author's ability to continue creating helpful resources

- Respect copyright and intellectual property laws

We want everyone who needs this workbook to have their own copy—
a private space for their personal journey.

If You Want to Share This Work

Ways to Share Without Violating Copyright

- **Gift the book:** Buy copies for friends or family who might benefit

- **Share your story:** Talk about how the workbook helped you (without reproducing content)

- **Recommend it:** Write reviews, tell your therapist, suggest it insupport groups

- **Create your own content:** Write about your journey inspired by thiswork

- **Request library copies:** Ask your local library to carry it

For Therapists and Professionals

If you're a mental health professional who wants to use this workbook with clients:

- **Each client needs their own copy** for privacy and personal use

- **You may reference exercises** but not reproduce them

- **Group use requires written permission** from the publisher

- **Professional bulk discounts** may be available - contact phlabs.org

Final Privacy Reminder

This workbook is your private sanctuary.

What you write here is sacred and secret.
Your patterns, your discoveries, your healing—
all of it belongs to you alone.

You decide what to share and when.

Until then, this is just between you and these pages.

WORKBOOK USE AGREEMENT

PLEASE READ CAREFULLY BEFORE USING THIS WORKBOOK

This agreement outlines important information about using *From Chains to Wings: The Workbook*. By using this workbook, you acknowledge that you have read, understood, and agree to these terms.

Understanding the Nature of This Workbook

This workbook IS:

- A self-help tool based on the author's personal experience and observations

- A collection of exercises some people find helpful

- A companion to personal growth and awareness

- Meant to be used at your own pace and discretion

This workbook IS NOT:

- A substitute for professional medical or mental health treatment

- Therapy, counseling, or clinical intervention

- A diagnostic tool

- Appropriate for crisis intervention

- Guaranteed to work for everyone

ASSUMPTION OF RISK

By using this workbook, you acknowledge that:

- **Some exercises may increase emotional distress** for certain individuals

- **Working with trauma-related patterns** can temporarily intensify symptoms

- **Individual responses vary significantly** and cannot be predicted

- **The author cannot anticipate** your unique circumstances or reactions

You voluntarily assume all risks associated with using these exercises.

Your Responsibilities as a User

By using this workbook, I understand and agree that:

☐ I will **skip any exercise** that increases my distress or feels unsafe

☐ I will **seek professional help** if my symptoms worsen or if I experience crisis

☐ I will **not use this workbook as my only support** if I have diagnosed mental health conditions

☐ I will **take breaks** whenever needed and not force myself through exercises

☐ I will **consult healthcare providers** about any physical or mental health concerns

☐ I understand that **progress is not guaranteed** and patterns may persist despite practice

SAFETY COMMITMENTS

I agree to prioritize my safety by:

- Stopping any exercise that feels overwhelming
- Calling 988 or going to an emergency room if I have thoughts of self-harm
- Working with a therapist if exercises consistently trigger strong reactions
- Being honest with myself about my capacity and limitations
- Treating myself with compassion when exercises don't help

Limitations of Liability

You expressly agree that:

- The author and publisher are **not liable** for any direct, indirect, incidental, or consequential damages resulting from your use of this workbook
- The author **makes no warranties** about the effectiveness of these exercises
- You are **fully responsible** for your physical and mental wellbeing while using this workbook
- You will **not hold the author or publisher responsible** for any outcomes, positive or negative
- This limitation applies even if you experience adverse effects from the exercises

Professional Support

You agree to seek professional help immediately if you experience:

- Thoughts of self-harm or suicide
- Inability to care for yourself (eating, sleeping, hygiene)
- Severe dissociation or feeling disconnected from reality
- Panic attacks that won't subside
- Any symptoms that significantly interfere with daily functioning

INFORMED CONSENT

By using this workbook, you confirm that:

- You are using this workbook **voluntarily**

- You understand its **limitations and risks**

- You accept **full responsibility** for your decision to use it

- You will **prioritize your safety** over completing exercises

- You have **access to crisis resources** if needed (988, 911, etc.)

ACKNOWLEDGMENT OF AGREEMENT

By beginning to use this workbook, I acknowledge that I have read, understood, and agree to all terms in this agreement. I understand that this is a binding agreement that affects my legal rights.

Name (optional): _____

Date started: _____

If you do not agree to these terms, please do not use this workbook.

Remember: Your safety and wellbeing come first.

No exercise is worth compromising your mental or physical health.

When in doubt, seek professional support.